STUDENT'S BOOK 2

B1

Herbert Puchta, Jeff Stranks & Peter Lewis-Jones

CONTENTS

Welcome p 4 **A** Introducing yourself; Answering questions; The weather; Families **B** Meeting people; Irregular past participles; losing things; furniture
C Buying and talking about food; In a restaurant; Shops; Things you have to do **D** Plans and arrangements; Sports and sport verbs; Travel plans

	FUNCTIONS & SPEAKING	GRAMMAR	VOCABULARY
Unit 1 Amazing people p 12	Talking about things you have and haven't done Offering encouragement Role play: Good causes	Present perfect with *just*, *already* and *yet* Present perfect vs. past simple	Personality adjectives Collocations **WordWise**: Phrases with *just*
Unit 2 The ways we learn p 20	Asking and giving / refusing permission Role play: Asking permission	Present perfect with *for* and *since* *a*, *an*, *the* or no article	School subjects Verbs about thinking
Review Units 1 & 2	pages 28–29		
Unit 3 That's entertainment p 30	Comparing things and actions Asking for and offering help	Comparative and superlative adjectives (review) (not) *as* .... *as* comparatives Making a comparison stronger or weaker Adverbs and comparative adverbs	Types of films Types of TV programmes **WordWise**: Expressions with *get*
Unit 4 Social networking p 38	Giving advice	Indefinite pronouns (*everyone*, *no one*, *someone*, etc.) *all* / *some* / *none* / *any of them* *should(n't)*, *had better*, *ought to*	IT terms Language for giving advice
Review Units 3 & 4	pages 46–47		
Unit 5 My life in music p 48	Asking about feelings Role play: Helpful suggestions	Present perfect continuous Present perfect simple vs. present perfect continuous	Making music Musical instruments **WordWise**: Phrasal verbs with *out*
Unit 6 Making a difference p 56	Expressing surprise and enthusiasm	*will* (not), *may* (not), *might* (not) for prediction First conditional *unless* in first conditional sentences	The environment Verbs to talk about energy
Review Units 5 & 6	pages 64–65		
Unit 7 Future fun p 66	Checking information Agreeing	Future forms Question tags *Nor/Neither* / *So*	Future time expressions Arranging a party **WordWise**: Phrases with *about*
Unit 8 Science counts p 74	Talking about past habits Talking about imaginary situations Talking about scientific discoveries	Past simple vs. past continuous (review) *used to* Second conditional *I wish*	Direction and movement Science
Review Units 7 & 8	pages 82–83		
Unit 9 What a job! p 84	Accepting and refusing invitations Role play: Inviting friends to join you	The passive (present simple, past simple, present continuous, present perfect)	Jobs *work as* / *in* / *for* *work* vs. *job* **WordWise**: Time expressions with *in*
Unit 10 Keep healthy p 92	Talking about your health	Past perfect simple Past perfect continuous Past perfect simple vs. past perfect continuous	Time linkers Illness: collocations
Review Units 9 & 10	pages 100–101		
Unit 11 Making the news p 102	Reporting what someone has said Expressing feelings: anger	Reported statements Verb patterns: object + infinitive	Fun More verbs with object + infinitive **WordWise**: Expressions with *make*
Unit 12 Playing by the rules p 110	Talking about permission Following and giving simple instructions	*be allowed to* / *let* Third conditional	Discipline Talking about consequences and reasons
Review Units 11 & 12	pages 118–119		

Pronunciation   pages 120–121   **Get it right!**   pages 122–126   **Speaking activities**   pages 127–128

PRONUNCIATION	THINK	SKILLS
Intonation and sentence stress	**Values:** Human qualities **Self-esteem:** Personal qualities	Reading Online survey responses: Who do you admire most? TV programme preview: Britain's Smartest Kids Photostory: The new café Writing A short passage about someone you admire Listening Playing a guessing game
Word stress	**Values:** Learning for life **Train to Think:** Learning about texts	Reading Article: An education like no other Article: Learning is brain change Culture: A day in the life of … Writing An email describing your school routine Listening Conversation about a book
Words ending in /ə/	**Values:** Spending wisely **Self-esteem:** The film of my life	Reading Article: Big movies on a small budget TV listings: different types of programmes Photostory: Extras Writing A paragraph about your TV habits Listening Interview with a teenage filmmaker
The short /ʌ/ vowel sound	**Values:** Responsible online behaviour **Train to Think:** Logical sequencing	Reading Article: Think before you act online Short texts: Different types of messages Culture: Communication through history Writing A web page giving advice Listening Conversation about installing a computer game
Been: strong /biːn/ and weak /bɪn/	**Values:** Following your dreams **Self-esteem:** Music and me	Reading Online forum: Singer songwriter: Any advice? Article: John Otway – Rock's greatest failure Photostory: Pop in the park Writing The story of your favourite band Listening Interviews about music
/f/, /v/ and /b/ consonant sounds	**Values:** Caring for the world **Train to Think:** Different perspectives	Reading Article: Hot topic: The environment Leaflet: Small changes, BIG consequences Culture: Stop! Before it's too late Writing An article for the school magazine Listening Interviews about a town project
Intonation of question tags	**Values:** Believe in a better future **Self-esteem:** Personal goals	Reading Newspaper articles: The world today Web chat: arranging a party Photostory: Weekend plans Writing An invitation Listening Interviews with two newsmakers
The /juː/ sound	**Values:** How science helps people **Train to Think:** Using criteria	Reading Blog article: Why aren't people more interested in science? Web forum: What should science do next? Culture: Great scientists Writing A blog entry Listening The things kids believe!
/tʃ/ and /dʒ/ consonant sounds	**Values:** What's important in a job? **Self-esteem:** I'd rather be …	Reading Article: Dream jobs Article: Obsolete jobs Photostory: For a good cause Writing A short essay about jobs that will soon be obsolete Listening People with disabilities and their jobs
/tʃ/ and /ʃ/ consonant sounds	**Values:** Never give up **Train to Think:** About health	Reading Article: 8,000 birds to see before you die Article: Miracle operations Culture: Keeping healthy – stories from around the world Writing A story about a sports event Listening A presentation on the benefits of exercise
Intonation: rude or polite?	**Values:** Being able to laugh at yourself **Self-esteem:** Giving an award	Reading Article: April Fool's Day Article: A tale of two Guys Photostory: The journalist Writing A news report Listening Profile on an extreme weather journalist
Silent consonants	**Values:** The importance of rules **Train to Think:** Play *rock, paper, scissors*	Reading Article: Hard times to be a kid Website contest: The best 50-word stories Culture: Strange laws around the world Writing A set of rules Listening The game *rock, paper, scissors*

WELCOME

A GETTING TO KNOW YOU
Introducing yourself

1 Read the letter quickly. Write the names under the photos.

Hi Paulo,

My name's Nicola and I'd like to be your pen pal. I got your name from my teacher, Miss Edwards. She lived in Brazil for three years, and she's a good friend of your mother's.

So what would you like to know about me? I'm 15 years old. I live in a small house in Manchester with my mum and my two little brothers. They're OK, but they can be annoying sometimes. I go to Bluecoat High School. I quite like school, but my teachers always give us too much homework. I usually do it when I get home from school, but I'm not doing that today – that's because I'm writing to you!

I like listening to music and playing games on the computer. I also like playing the guitar. I play in a band with some of my friends. I like sport, too. I play volleyball and tennis. I'm in the school tennis team. We usually play matches on Saturday mornings. That's a bit of a problem because I don't really like getting up early at the weekend.

But what about you? I hope you'll want to write to me. There are lots of questions I want to ask you. Things like: what's life like in Brazil? Do you like your school? What's it like? What's the weather like in Rio? Have you got a big family? All that sort of stuff, to help me get to know you. Miss Edwards says you like surfing, but that's all I know about you.

So please write. I'd love to have a Brazilian friend.

Best

Nicola

2 Read the letter and complete the form about Nicola.

Name _Nicola_   Hometown _____
Age _____   Family _____
Likes _____
Dislikes _____

Asking questions

3 Match the questions with the answers to make mini-dialogues.

1. What do you do?
2. What are you doing?
3. What do you like doing?
4. Do you like studying English?
5. Where are you from?
6. Are you 14?

a. I'm watching TV.
b. Yes, it's great.
c. I'm from Italy.
d. I'm a student.
e. No, I'm 13.
f. I love playing tennis.

4 **SPEAKING** Work in pairs. Ask and answer the questions in Exercise 3. Give answers that are true for you.

5 Choose the next line for each of the mini-dialogues in Exercise 3.

1. What's your teacher's name?
2. Do you live in Rome?
3. What school do you go to?
4. When is your birthday?
5. Would you like to go out and do something with me?
6. Me too. Do you want to come over and play the new Angry Birds game?

6 **SPEAKING** Work in pairs. Think of one more line for each dialogue. Then practise your dialogues.

What do you do?   *I'm a student.*

What school do you go to?

St Mark's High School in York.

WELCOME

Miami

Rio

London

Oslo

Istanbul

The weather

1 What kind of weather do you love, like or hate? Draw a ☺, ☺ or a ☹ next to each one.

- ☐ sunny ◯
- ☐ wet ◯
- ☐ cloudy ◯
- ☐ warm ◯
- ☐ cold ◯
- ☐ windy ◯
- ☐ humid ◯
- ☐ rainy ◯
- ☐ dry ◯
- ☐ freezing ◯
- ☐ hot ◯
- ☐ foggy ◯

2 **SPEAKING** Work in pairs. Tell your partner.

I love rainy weather.

3 🔊 1.02 Listen to the weather forecast for the UK. Tick (✓) the weather words in Exercise 1 that you hear.

4 🔊 1.02 Listen again. What is the weather going to be like in Manchester, Birmingham and London?

5 **SPEAKING** Work in pairs. Look at the pictures. Ask and answer questions.

What's the weather like in Miami?

It's windy and very wet.

Families

1 Look at the family words. Complete the pairs.

1 mother and _____   4 grandma and _____
2 brother and _____   5 husband and _____
3 aunt and _____   6 cousin and _____

2 🔊 1.03 Listen to Nicola talking to Paulo on Skype. How are these people related to Nicola?

1 Colin _____   6 Mike _____
2 Luke _____   7 Jamie _____
3 Sharon _____   8 Kai _____
4 Becky _____   9 Shay _____
5 Jodie _____   10 Joe _____

3 **SPEAKING** Work in pairs. Ask each other about your families.

Have you got any cousins?

What's your uncle's name?

B EXPERIENCES
Meeting people

1 Put the parts of dialogue in order. Write 1–10 in the boxes.

- [ ] A Really! Where? When?
- [ ] A What book was it?
- [ ] A Did he give you one?
- [1] A Have you ever met a famous person?
- [ ] A Did you say anything to him?
- [ ] B It was my English course book, believe it or not. I had it with me to help me with my English.
- [ ] B Yes, he was really nice. I didn't have any paper with me, so he signed a book that I was carrying.
- [ ] B It was last summer. We were on holiday in LA. We were walking out of a restaurant when he walked in.
- [ ] B Yes, I did. I asked him for an autograph.
- [ ] B Yes, I have. Bradley Cooper.

2 🔊 1.04 Listen and check.

3 **SPEAKING** Work with a partner. Practise the conversation. Change names, places and other details.

4 <u>Underline</u> examples of the following tenses in Exercise 1.
1 A past simple positive statement.
2 A past simple negative statement.
3 A past simple question.
4 A past simple short answer.
5 A past continuous statement.
6 A present perfect question with *ever*.
7 A present perfect short answer.

Irregular past participles

1 Write the past participles of these irregular verbs.

1 think _____   7 eat _____
2 drink _____   8 make _____
3 wear _____   9 run _____
4 see _____   10 win _____
5 lose _____   11 read _____
6 hear _____   12 ride _____

2 Complete the questions with eight of the past participles in Exercise 1.
1 Who's the most famous person you've ever *seen* ?
2 What's the strangest food you've ever _____ ?
3 What's the best book you've ever _____ ?
4 What's the funniest joke you've ever _____ ?
5 What's the most expensive thing you've ever _____ and never found again?
6 What's the best prize you've ever _____ ?
7 What are the most embarrassing clothes you've ever _____ ?
8 What's the longest phone call you've ever _____ ?

3 Answer the questions in Exercise 2 with your own information. Give details.

The most famous person I've ever seen is Lionel Messi.

4 Work in groups of eight. Each person takes one of the questions from Exercise 2 and thinks of two more questions to ask.

Who's the most famous person you've ever seen?
Where did you see him/her?
Did you say anything to him/her?

5 **SPEAKING** Ask the other students in your group your questions.

6 **SPEAKING** Report back to the group.

The most famous person Carla has seen is Lionel Messi. She saw him outside a shop in Barcelona. She didn't say anything to him.

Losing things

1 Read the story and find the answer to the question.

What was in the wrong container?

> People often complain about airline companies losing their suitcases when they fly. It's never happened to me, but something a lot worse happened to my family recently.
>
> About ten years ago my mum got a job teaching at a university in Indonesia. At first she only went for six months, but she really liked it and agreed to stay longer, so we all went to live with her. We had a great time, but last year my parents decided that they wanted to return to the UK. Because we'd been there so long we had loads of things we wanted to take back with us – all the furniture from our house in fact.
>
> So mum and dad went to a shipping company and arranged to take everything back in one of those big containers that you see on ships. The company packed everything into it: the armchair and sofas, the TV, wardrobes, desks, even all the carpets and curtains. Our whole house was inside that big green metal box.
>
> We flew back to the UK and waited for the container to arrive. About ten weeks later we were having breakfast one morning when a big lorry arrived outside our house. On the back was a big green metal box. We were so excited. The men opened the container and started to take out our things. But they weren't our things. The container was full of motorbikes. It was the wrong one. My parents were so annoyed. But the story has a happy ending. The men took the container and motorbikes away, and about two months ago our things finally arrived.

2 Read the story again and answer the questions. Use the word in brackets in your answer.

1. When did Liam's mum start her job in Indonesia? (ago)
2. When did the family move to Indonesia? (later)
3. How long did they stay there? (about)
4. When did they decide to move back to the UK? (last)
5. How long after they were back in the UK did the first container arrive? (about)
6. When did the correct container finally arrive? (ago)

3 **WRITING** Write a short story about something you lost. Use these questions to help you.

- When did it happen?
- What was it?
- Where did you lose it?
- What did you do?
- How did you feel?
- Did you find it? If so, when and where?

Furniture

1 Tick (✓) the items mentioned in the story.

2 **SPEAKING** Name the other items. Which of these do you think Liam's parents probably didn't put into the container?

> They probably didn't put the toilet into the container.

3 Discuss in small groups.

Your family is moving to the other side of the world. They are packing the house things into a container, but there is only room for five items. What five items of furniture from your house are you going to choose?

C EATING AND DRINKING
Buying and talking about food

1 🔊 1.05 Listen and complete each space with one word.

ASSISTANT	Morning, can I help you?
CUSTOMER	Yes, please. Um, I want ¹_____ onions.
ASSISTANT	OK, how many?
CUSTOMER	Two kilos. And can I have ²_____ mushrooms too, please? About half a kilo?
ASSISTANT	OK. Anything ³_____ ?
CUSTOMER	Oh, yes – tomatoes. A kilo of tomatoes, please. And ⁴_____ olives.
ASSISTANT	Sorry, we haven't got ⁵_____ olives today. Try the ⁶_____ across the street.
CUSTOMER	OK, thanks.
ASSISTANT	Here are your tomatoes. So, are you going to make pizza tonight with all this?
CUSTOMER	No, I'm not. I'm making '⁷_____ à la grecque'. It's a French dish. I had it on holiday in France. I loved it!
ASSISTANT	What about lemons? You don't ⁸_____ to put lemon juice in it, but it's a ⁹_____ good idea!
CUSTOMER	Oh, right. No, it's OK, thanks. I've ¹⁰_____ got lemons at home. So how ¹¹_____ is that?
ASSISTANT	Let's see. That's £4.35, please.
CUSTOMER	Here you are – £5.
ASSISTANT	And 65p ¹²_____ . Thanks. Enjoy your dinner!

2 Complete each sentence with *some* or *any*. Then match the sentences with the pictures. Write the numbers 1–8.

1 There's _____ yoghurt in the fridge.
2 There are _____ mushrooms in the kitchen.
3 There aren't _____ mushrooms in the pizza.
4 I'd like _____ of those potatoes, please.
5 Sorry, there aren't _____ potatoes.
6 I'd like _____ coffee, please.
7 Oh, there isn't _____ yoghurt.
8 No, I don't want _____ coffee, thanks.

3 **SPEAKING** Which of these things would you always / never / sometimes see on a pizza?

carrots | onions | peppers | yoghurt | pears
pineapple | chicken | mushrooms | tomatoes
cheese | olives

There's always cheese on a pizza – but you never see ... !

4 **ROLE PLAY** Work in pairs. Use your sentences from Exercise 3 to do a role play.

WELCOME

In a restaurant

1 🔊 1.06 Read the sentences. Mark them W (waitress) or C (customer). Listen and check.

1 Can we see the menu, please?
2 Is everything OK?
3 There's too much salt in the soup!
4 The bill, please.
5 A table for two? This way, please.
6 We'd both like the fish, please. And the soup to start.
7 It's very noisy here. There are too many people.
8 Are you ready to order?

2 Complete each phrase with *much* or *many*.

1 too _____ sugar
2 too _____ salt
3 too _____ mushrooms
4 too _____ money
5 too _____ people
6 too _____ things on the menu

3 Complete the mini-dialogues with a phrase from Exercise 2.

1 A This soup is horrible.
  B I know! There's _____ in it.
2 A Ugh! I can't drink this coffee.
  B I know! There's _____ in it.
3 A This pizza isn't so good.
  B I know! I like mushrooms, but there are _____ on it!
4 A This is horrible. We can't talk.
  B I know! There are _____ here.
5 A I don't know what to choose.
  B I know! There are _____ .
6 A Look! €30.00 for a pizza!!
  B I know! It's _____ .

Shops

1 Look at the shops below. What things can you buy in each place? Think of as many things as you can.

newsagent's ☐   shoe shop ☐
chemist's ☐   post office ☐
bookshop ☐   supermarket ☐
clothes shop ☐   sports shop ☐

2 🔊 1.07 Listen. Which shop is each person in? Write the number of the dialogue next to the correct shop in Exercise 1. There are three shops you won't need.

3 🔊 1.07 Listen again. In which shop do you hear these words?

1 You don't have to wait in a queue. _____
2 You have to wear them two or three times. _____
3 You don't have to buy a larger size than you need. _____
4 You have to fill in this form. _____
5 You don't have to pay for the third one. _____

Things you have to do

1 Read the sentences below. For each one, think of possibilities for a) who said it and b) who to.

1 *You don't have to eat it.*
2 *You have to give it to me tomorrow morning.*
3 *I don't have to listen to you!*
4 *I have to finish this tonight.*
5 *You don't have to put mushrooms on it.*
6 *It's fantastic! I have to buy it!*

2 **SPEAKING** Work in pairs. Choose three of the sentences in Exercise 1. Act out a mini-dialogue for each sentence that you choose.

Chicken? Again? That's boring.

Well, you don't have to eat it.

Can I have something else?

No, we've only got chicken.

OK then – I'll eat the chicken.

Hi Susana

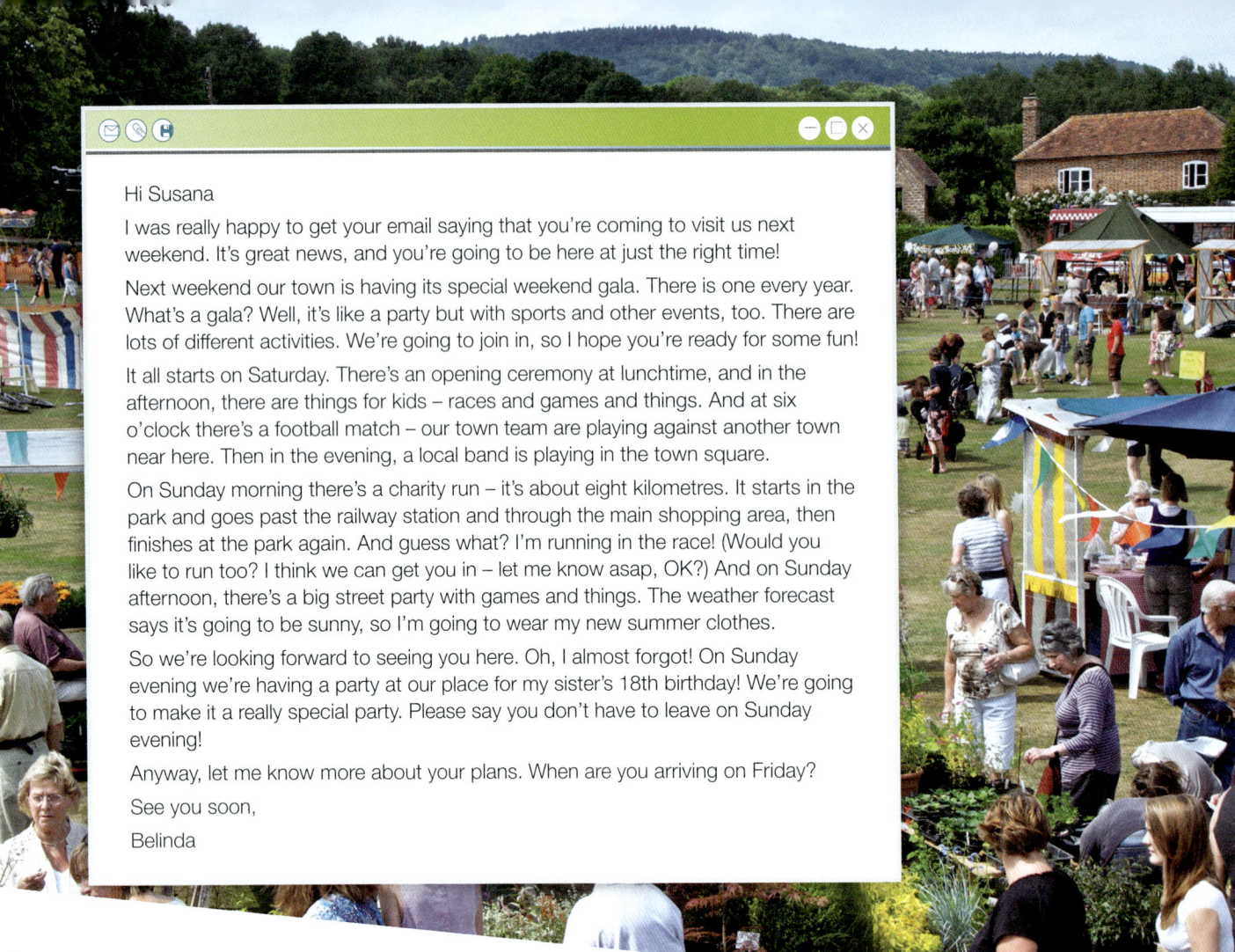

I was really happy to get your email saying that you're coming to visit us next weekend. It's great news, and you're going to be here at just the right time!

Next weekend our town is having its special weekend gala. There is one every year. What's a gala? Well, it's like a party but with sports and other events, too. There are lots of different activities. We're going to join in, so I hope you're ready for some fun!

It all starts on Saturday. There's an opening ceremony at lunchtime, and in the afternoon, there are things for kids – races and games and things. And at six o'clock there's a football match – our town team are playing against another town near here. Then in the evening, a local band is playing in the town square.

On Sunday morning there's a charity run – it's about eight kilometres. It starts in the park and goes past the railway station and through the main shopping area, then finishes at the park again. And guess what? I'm running in the race! (Would you like to run too? I think we can get you in – let me know asap, OK?) And on Sunday afternoon, there's a big street party with games and things. The weather forecast says it's going to be sunny, so I'm going to wear my new summer clothes.

So we're looking forward to seeing you here. Oh, I almost forgot! On Sunday evening we're having a party at our place for my sister's 18th birthday! We're going to make it a really special party. Please say you don't have to leave on Sunday evening!

Anyway, let me know more about your plans. When are you arriving on Friday?

See you soon,

Belinda

D LOOKING AHEAD

Plans and arrangements

1 Read the email. Match the times and the events.

1 Saturday lunchtime
2 Saturday afternoon
3 Saturday evening
4 Sunday morning
5 Sunday afternoon
6 Sunday evening

a kids' games and races
b party for Belinda's sister
c opening ceremony
d local band
e charity run
f street party

2 Read the sentences. What do the underlined verbs express? Write A (arrangement) or I (intention).

1 In the evening, a local band <u>is playing</u> in the town square.
2 <u>I'm running</u> in the race.
3 <u>We're going to join in</u>.
4 <u>I'm going to wear</u> my new summer clothes.
5 <u>We're going to make</u> it a really special party.
6 <u>We're having</u> a party at our place.

3 <u>Underline</u> other examples of present continuous for arrangements in Belinda's email.

4 SPEAKING Work in pairs. Ask and answer questions about plans you have for next weekend.

What are you doing on Saturday morning?

I'm going running. / I'm not doing anything. Why?

Sports and sport verbs

1 Complete the table with the sports in the list.

running | football | tennis | gymnastics
athletics | rock climbing | karate | skiing

play	do	go

2 SPEAKING Work in pairs. Which sports do you do often / sometimes / never? Talk to your partner.

I often go running, but I never do karate.

WELCOME

Travel plans

1 🔊 1.08 Put the parts of the dialogue in order. Then listen and check.

- [ ] A Great idea. OK, see you soon. We're going to have a lot of fun this weekend!
- [ ] A Oh dear, 5.30 is difficult for me. Is it OK if I don't meet you at the station?
- [1] A Hey, Susana. What time are you arriving on Friday?
- [ ] A Well, sometimes the train's late. If it's late, I'll meet you.
- [ ] B OK. As soon as the train leaves London, I'll send you a text message.
- [ ] B 5.30 – I'm going to catch the four o'clock train from London.
- [ ] B I know. It's going to be great!
- [ ] B Of course. I can take a taxi. No problem.

2 Complete the sentences with the correct form of the verbs in brackets.

1. If I _____ (miss) the train, I _____ (catch) the next one.
2. If the train _____ (arrive) late, I _____ (take) a taxi.
3. If there _____ (not be) any taxis, I _____ (walk) to your place.
4. I'll send you a text message when I _____ (get) to the station.
5. As soon as I _____ (get) to your place, we _____ (start) having a good time.
6. If we _____ (not have) a good time, I _____ (not visit) you again!

3 Lola travelled a lot last year. Complete the sentences with the past simple of the verbs in the list.

~~take~~ | catch | drive | fly | miss | ride

4 Complete the sentences with *be going to* and the verbs in the list.

visit | take | not visit | get up | try | buy

1. We don't like flying so we _____ a train.
2. I want to go to New York. I _____ my ticket online.
3. My plane leaves at 6.00, so I _____ very early tomorrow.
4. We'll only be in Paris for one day, so we _____ any museums.
5. When we're in London, we _____ my cousins.
6. We love Spanish food, so we _____ all the best restaurants in Madrid!

5 Imagine you can take a holiday wherever you want, any time you want. Make notes about your plans:
- where you're going to go
- where you're going to stay
- how long your holiday is going to be
- what you're going to do
- who you're going to go with
- what you're going to eat
- what time of year you're going to go

6 **SPEAKING** Work in pairs. Ask and answer about the holiday you planned in Exercise 5.

Where are you going to go on holiday?

New York. And I'm going to stay in an expensive hotel.

0 She _took_ a taxi in Paris.

1 She _____ the train in Munich.

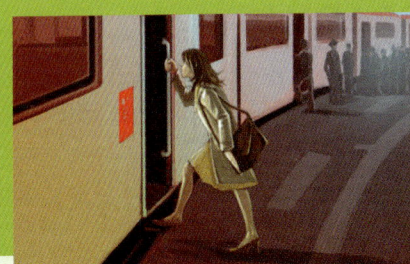
2 She _____ the train in Vienna.

3 She _____ to Rome.

4 She _____ to Madrid.

5 She _____ a bike in Athens.

1 AMAZING PEOPLE

OBJECTIVES

FUNCTIONS: talking about things you have and haven't done; offering encouragement
GRAMMAR: present perfect with *just*, *already* and *yet*; present perfect vs. past simple
VOCABULARY: personality adjectives; collocations; phrases with *just*

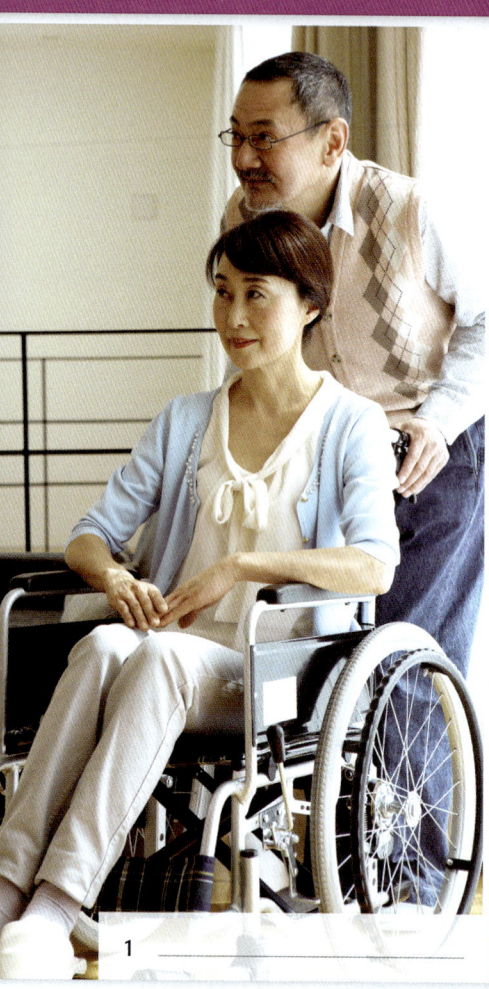

1 _____

2 _____

3 _____

4 _____

READING

1 Look at the photos. What is your first impression of these people? What adjectives could you use to describe them?

caring | friendly | boring | serious | cheerful
funny | intelligent | cool | confident | easy-going

2 **SPEAKING** Discuss the photos in pairs.

> He seems friendly.
>
> She looks like a cheerful person because she's smiling.

3 **SPEAKING** Use the adjectives in Exercise 1 and other adjectives to describe people you know. Give reasons.

> My brother is very easy-going. He doesn't get angry very often.

4 Read the responses to an online survey quickly. Write the name of each person under the photos.

5 🔊 1.09 Read and listen to the responses again. Mark the sentences T (true) or F (false). Correct the false information.

1 Mrs Marconi has a dangerous job. ___
2 She isn't very popular with Bia's friends. ___
3 Mr Donaldson has a problem controlling his students. ___
4 Jacob thinks Mr Donaldson will be famous one day. ___
5 Alex's grandmother is older than she looks. ___
6 Gwen thinks it's important to enjoy life. ___
7 Oliver's aunt had a car accident. ___
8 Oliver's uncle changed after the accident. ___

12

WHO DO YOU ADMIRE MOST?

`Popular` `Recent`

Jackie, 14 ★ Sofia Marconi, my friend Bia's mum, is probably the most amazing person I know. She's also extremely **brave**. She's a wildlife photographer and she travels to some of the most dangerous places on Earth to take photos of the world's most endangered animals. She's just come back from Papua New Guinea. I haven't seen her photos yet, but I bet they're amazing. She's quite famous and she's already been on TV. Although she spends quite a bit of time away from home, she's also a really cool mum. She's really **charming** and all of Bia's friends think she's fab. Bia's really lucky to have such a great mum.

Jacob, 16 One of my heroes is Mr Donaldson, our music teacher. First of all, he's a brilliant teacher. He's really **laid-back** but we all respect him, and no one ever messes about in his class. He's so **creative** and finds different ways to get us interested in his lessons. He's also a really amazing guitar player – I mean he is seriously **talented**. He's in a band. They haven't made any recordings yet, but they've already attracted lots of interest and I'm sure they're going to be famous one day. I'll be really happy for him, but I hope it doesn't happen too soon. I don't want to lose my teacher!

Alex, 15 The person I admire more than anyone is my grandmother Gwen. She's 78 and looks just amazing. Many people think she's my mother when they see us together. But she doesn't just *look* young, she *is* young. She's one of the most **active** people I know. She spends a lot of her time doing things for charity. For example, she's just done a parachute jump to raise money for a children's charity in India. A parachute jump! At her age! She's such a **positive** person, always seeing the good in other people. 'Life is for living,' she tells me. I hope I have that much life in me when I'm her age.

Oliver, 17 ★ The greatest person I know is my uncle Jack. He and my aunt Alice had the perfect life: good jobs, a lovely house and three young children. Then one day their life changed forever. My aunt had a terrible car accident. It left her in a wheelchair. From that day on, my uncle has devoted his time to looking after her and the family. But I have never heard him complain. He's still the same lovely person he always was. I know life is hard for him but he's always so **cheerful** with a huge smile on his face. He's such a warm person – someone you want to spend time with.

1 AMAZING PEOPLE

6 **VOCABULARY** There are eight words in bold in the texts. Match the words with these meanings. Write the words.

0 is always doing things _active_
1 is usually happy _____
2 is very easy-going _____
3 has very original ideas _____
4 looks for the good in all situations _____
5 is very good at doing something _____
6 doesn't get scared easily _____
7 is very easy to like _____

7 Complete the sentences with the words from Exercise 6.

0 Why are you so _cheerful_ today? Have you had some good news?
1 He stood up in the front of the whole school and read out his poem. He was really _____ .
2 She's very _____ and it's easy to see why she's got so many friends.
3 He's so _____ that some people think he's a bit lazy.
4 Have you seen him doing ballet? He really is a _____ dancer.
5 If you want to work in advertising, you need to be _____ and come up with really good ideas.
6 My dad is really _____ around the house. He's always cooking or fixing things or working in the garden.
7 He's had a really difficult life but he's really _____ about the future.

THiNK VALUES

Human qualities

1 Think about someone who is not famous but who you think is special.

a Think of three adjectives to describe them.
b Think about why you chose these adjectives. Make notes.

2 **SPEAKING** Tell your partner about the person you admire.

> *I really admire my brother. He's really confident in difficult situations.*

13

GRAMMAR

Present perfect with *just*, *already* and *yet*

1 Complete the example sentences with *just*, *already* and *yet*. Then complete the rules with the missing words.

1 She's _____ come back from Papua New Guinea.
2 They haven't made any recordings _____ , but they've _____ attracted a lot of interest.

> **RULE:** In the present perfect, we often use
> - ¹_____ in negative sentences and questions to talk about something that hasn't happened but that we expect to happen soon. It comes at the end of the sentence.
> - ²_____ to emphasise that something happened very recently. It goes before the past participle.
> - ³_____ to show that something has been done or finished sooner than expected. It usually goes before the past participle.

2 Match the pictures and the sentences. Write 1–3 in the boxes.

1 He's just finished his painting.
2 He's already sold the painting.
3 He hasn't finished his painting yet.

3 Look at Mike's list of things to do for his party. Write sentences with *already* and *yet*.

1 *He hasn't made the cake yet.*

4 Use your imagination to answer the questions. Use the present perfect and *just* in each one.

1 Why is Mum so angry?
   Because Dad's just crashed her car.
2 Why is Colin so sad?
3 Why is your face so dirty?
4 What's Liam so scared about?
5 Why is Dana so excited?
6 Why are you smiling?

5 Tick (✓) the things you have already done.

6 **SPEAKING** Work in pairs. Ask each other questions.

> Have you started a blog yet?
>
> Yes, I've already done that. Have you?
>
> No, I haven't done that yet.

Workbook page 10

1 AMAZING PEOPLE

LISTENING

1 🔊 1.10 Listen to some people playing a game called Mystery Guest. How many people are playing?

2 🔊 1.10 Listen again. For each question there are three pictures. Choose the correct picture and put a tick (✓) in the box below it.

1 What does Will's mystery guest do?

A ☐   B ☐   C ☐

2 Where is Will's mystery guest from?

A ☐   B ☐   C ☐

3 Who does Will think Kiki's mystery guest is?

A ☐   B ☐   C ☐

4 What does Kiki's mystery guest do?

A ☐   B ☐   C ☐

3 🔊 1.10 Work in pairs. Answer the questions. Then listen again and check.

1 Who is Will's mystery guest?
2 What adjectives does Will use to describe him?
3 Who is Kiki's mystery guest?
4 What adjectives does Kiki use to describe her?

4 **SPEAKING** Work in pairs. Play Mystery Guest.

Ladies and gentlemen, my guest is ...

He/She has won / played / recorded / helped ...

THiNK SELF-ESTEEM

Personal qualities

1 A cinquain is a short, five-line poem. Read the cinquain and complete the rules with the words in the list.

Kiki
Charming, creative
Sings – laughs – loves
Talented
A beautiful voice

adjectives | three | verbs
someone's name | adjective

On the first line write ¹_____ .
On the second line write two ²_____ to describe the person.
On the third line write three ³_____ to show what the person likes doing.
On the fourth line write another ⁴_____ .
On the fifth line write a description of the person in just ⁵_____ words.

2 **WRITING** Write a cinquain about:

a your partner or best friend
b your hero

15

READING

1 **SPEAKING** Work in pairs. At what age did you learn to do these things?

- read
- draw
- play a musical instrument
- speak a foreign language

I learned to read when I was ...

I've never learned to ...

2 **SPEAKING** What other things have you learned in your life and when did you start to do them?

When I was seven I learned how to cook an omelette.

3 Read the TV programme preview quickly. Which of the children is a genius at these things? Write the names.

1 art _____
2 music _____
3 creative writing _____
4 languages _____

4 Read the programme preview again and answer the questions.

1 What writers did Mark enjoy when he was three?
2 What languages does he know?
3 How much will Daniel get for writing each book?
4 How many instruments does Samantha play?
5 How many weeks is the show on for?
6 Who will the show have interviews with?

Don't miss this week:

Britain's Smartest Kids

While other children were just starting their ABCs, three-year-old Mark Swallow was already reading Shakespeare and Charles Dickens. By the age of seven he was speaking fluent French and German and studying both Latin and Greek. Now, at the age of 12, Mark has just started a university degree in English literature.

Mark and other child geniuses will be the subject of a new documentary series which takes a look into the lives of these remarkable children and their families. In the programmes we will meet children like eight-year-old Daniel Manning, who wrote his first book when he was just five and who has just signed a £60,000 contract with a publishing house to write three novels. Then there is 12-year-old Samantha Price, who started piano lessons when she was three. Along with the piano, she now also plays the cello, clarinet and classical guitar. She has already played with three top European orchestras. And how about ten-year-old Jordan Welsh? She first picked up a paint brush before she could walk. She has already had an exhibition of her paintings in one of London's top art galleries and has just won a major prize for one of her paintings.

Over the next six weeks we will see what it is that makes these children so special. We will find out how and when their parents knew they were different and about the changes it made to their family life. We will hear from the children about their hopes and plans for the future. There are also interviews with former child geniuses, some who have gone on to great things and others who decided they wanted to return to a more normal life.

Join us Monday for the first documentary in this amazing series, **Britain's Smartest Kids**.

1 AMAZING PEOPLE

GRAMMAR
Present perfect vs. past simple

1 Look back at the review on page 16. Which questions can you answer with a specific point in time? Then complete the rules with *present perfect* or *past simple*.

1 When did Daniel write his first book?
2 When did he sign a £60,000 contract?
3 When did Samantha start piano lessons?
4 When did she play with orchestras?

> **RULE:** When we talk about a specific point in time in the past, we use the _____ .
> When we don't refer to a specific point in time, we often use the _____ .

2 Complete the pairs of sentences. Use the past simple and the present perfect of the verbs.

0 visit
  a I *have visited* Greece more than 20 times.
  b I first *visited* Greece in 1998.
1 win
  a He _____ already _____ three gold medals, and he hopes to win more.
  b He _____ a gold medal in the 2012 Olympics.
2 meet
  a My mum _____ a lot of interesting people in her life.
  b My mum _____ Prince Harry ten years ago.
3 do
  a Mum, I _____ my homework. Can I go out?
  b I _____ all the things on my to-do list before lunch!
4 record
  a They _____ their last album two years ago.
  b They _____ more than 20 albums so far.
5 live
  a We _____ in Samoa for three years when I was a teenager.
  b We're living in Austria now, but we _____ in many different countries.
6 sign
  a She _____ just _____ a contract with a new e-publishing company.
  b She _____ the contract for her first book on her 16th birthday.

> Workbook page 11

VOCABULARY
Collocations

1 Circle all the correct answers.
  1 Which of these can you sign?
    a a contract   b an autograph   c a lesson
  2 Which of these things can you write?
    a a novel   b a party   c a song
  3 Which of these things can you do?
    a a good time   b a degree   c something
  4 Which of these things can you win?
    a a prize   b a competition   c an exhibition
  5 Which of these can you make?
    a friends   b a cake   c homework
  6 Which of these can you miss?
    a a future   b your family   c the bus

2 What verbs can go before the six words you didn't circle in Exercise 1? Write at least one verb for each word.

3 **SPEAKING** Talk to other people in the class. Ask and answer questions and complete the table.

> Have you ever ... ? What happened?
>
> Who did you ask?
>
> What was the poem about?
>
> What did you win?

Find someone who has ...	Who?	Details
asked someone for an autograph.		
written a poem.		
had an interview.		
won a prize.		
made a cake.		
missed a train or a bus.		

> Workbook page 12

WRITING

Write a short passage about someone you have admired for some time. Include

- how long you have known them.
- what you admire about them.

PHOTOSTORY: episode 1

The new café

1 Look at the photos and answer the questions.

There is going to be a new café in the park.
Who does Luke think should open it?
Who does Ryan think should open it?

2 🔊 1.11 Now read and listen to the photostory. Check your answers.

LUKE Have you read this? They're opening a new café in the park. Saturday afternoon.
OLIVIA That's fantastic. Who's going to do the big opening ceremony?
RYAN The mayor probably. She always does shop openings and conferences, that sort of thing.
MEGAN They should get somebody more important.
LUKE What? More important than the mayor?

LUKE Hey, I know. They should get Paul Norris.
RYAN Yeah! He's a great footballer! He plays for United now, but he grew up round here.
OLIVIA But he doesn't live round here any more. He's a big star now. Let's face it, he won't want to open a little park café.
RYAN Yeah, you're probably right.

RYAN What about Paula Mayberry?
OLIVIA The actress from the soap opera, what's it called … *Linden Street*?
RYAN Yes.
MEGAN But why her? Did she live here once?
RYAN No, I don't think so. I'd just like to meet her.

LUKE Come on, there has to be somebody!
OLIVIA Look, the mayor is going to open the park café, and that's that.
RYAN I guess you're right. No one special lives in our town.
MEGAN Are you sure?
LUKE What do you mean?
MEGAN Know what, guys? I've just thought of someone *very* special, and he's just the person for the job.

1 AMAZING PEOPLE

DEVELOPING SPEAKING

3 Work in pairs. Discuss what happens next in the story. Write down your ideas.

We think the boys go and talk to Paul Norris, the footballer.

4 ⏯ EP1 Watch to find out how the story continues.

5 Complete the sentences with the words in the list.

Megan | the headmaster | the girls | Mr Lane
Olivia | the boys | the girls

1 Megan doesn't tell her idea to _____.
2 Megan shares her idea with _____.
3 Olivia offers to help _____.
4 The girls go to see _____.
5 The boys follow _____.
6 The mayor thanks. _____.
7 Olivia's special person is. _____.

PHRASES FOR FLUENCY

1 Find the expressions 1–6 in the story. Who says them? How do you say them in your language?

1 … that sort of thing.   *Ryan*
2 Let's face it, …   _____
3 I don't think so.   _____
4 … and that's that.   _____
5 Are you sure?   _____
6 Know what?   _____

2 Complete the conversations with the expressions in Exercise 1.

1 A That new girl, Sally – she likes you!
  B No, ¹_____ .
  A ²_____ ? I have a feeling she likes you a lot.
  B No. She never smiles at me. And she criticises me a lot, doesn't laugh at my jokes, ³_____ .

2 A Oh, you got it wrong again!
  B I know. ⁴_____ , I'm no good at computer games.
  A ⁵_____ ? We just need a rest. Let's go and watch some TV.
  B OK, but I don't want to play this game again, OK? I'm useless at it, ⁶_____ !

Pronunciation
Intonation and sentence stress
Go to page 120. 🔊

WordWise
Phrases with *just*

1 Look at the sentences from the unit. Choose the correct meaning of *just* in each one.

1 She's **just** come back from Papua New Guinea. ☐
2 He wrote his first book when he was **just** five. ☐
3 She's 78 and looks **just** amazing. ☐

a only
b a short time ago
c really

2 What does *just* mean in these sentences?

1 Don't be angry. It's just a joke.
2 I've just seen a fantastic film.
3 It's cold today. The weather is just awful.
4 No food, thanks – just a drink.
5 She's just had some bad news.

3 Match the questions to the answers.

1 How many spoons of sugar would you like? ☐
2 When did Jane get here? ☐
3 What do you think of Beyoncé? ☐

a She's just arrived.
b She's just great.
c Just one

➡ Workbook page 13

FUNCTIONS
Offering encouragement

1 ⏯ EP1 Watch the video again. Listen for sentences 1–5. Who says them? Why?

1 That is a great idea.
2 You should definitely do it.
3 You've got to make this happen.
4 I'll help you if you want.
5 Let's go and speak to some people.

Good causes

2 **ROLE PLAY** Work in pairs. Student A: go to page 127. Student B: go to page 128. Use the sentences from Exercise 1 to do the role play.

19

2 | THE WAYS WE LEARN

OBJECTIVES

FUNCTIONS: asking and giving / refusing permission to do something
GRAMMAR: present perfect with *for* and *since*; *a*, *an*, *the* or no article
VOCABULARY: school subjects; verbs about thinking

READING

1 Work in pairs. Write down words that come to mind when you think of these places.

a youth club | a holiday camp | a school

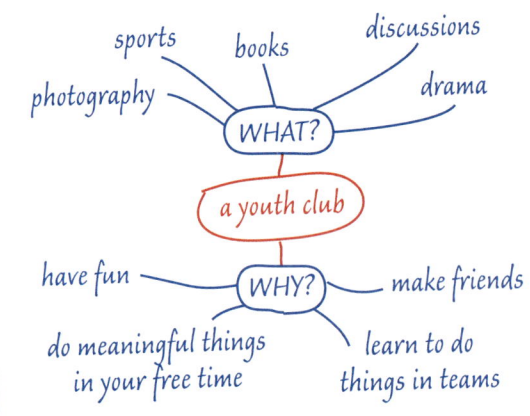

2 Look at the photos. What are the people doing? Where do you think they are?

3 🔊 1.14 Read and listen to the article. For each question, mark the correct letter A, B, C or D.

1 What is the writer doing in this text?
   A Describing a summer school he started in 2005.
   B Explaining how to send a child to Tinkering.
   C Talking about the US school system.
   D Talking about G. Tulley's programmes for kids.

2 What does the text say about safety at the school?
   A The school is too dangerous for kids.
   B No child has ever had an accident.
   C Children have never hurt themselves badly.
   D The school doesn't give information about that.

3 What reactions to Brightworks have there been in the media?
   A They have compared it to Tinkering School.
   B Most of them have been positive.
   C There hasn't been any reaction.
   D Most of them have been negative.

4 What effect has the school had on Tina Cooper?
   A It has changed her opinion about school.
   B It has given her exciting and boring times.
   C It has made her more interested in San Francisco.
   D It has encouraged her to ask more questions.

4 Which thing might Gever Tulley say in a presentation to parents about the Tinkering School?

   A We are trying to do our best. We offer your kids a balance of things they will like doing and things they will have to do.
   B I can guarantee that your son or daughter will learn to build a rollercoaster, a rope bridge, a tree house, a motorbike and a boat.
   C Kids can learn a lot by doing things in teams. We give them materials and tools. They plan and make things.
   D Most of the articles in newspapers and magazines say kids are more motivated here than at many other schools.

2 THE WAYS WE LEARN

An education like no other

Gever Tulley is a computer scientist from California. In 2005, he started a summer programme for children called Tinkering School. The idea was that children can learn important skills for life by building things together. Gever Tulley and his team help the children to think big and create plans for innovative things they want to build. Children have made fantastic things since the school started. They have built a rollercoaster. They have made a rope bridge from plastic shopping bags. They have made tree houses, wooden motorbikes and boats.

At Tinkering School, children get all kinds of materials like wood, metal, plastic, nails and ropes. They get lots of real tools too, such as knives, hammers, screwdrivers and power drills. Some children have cut themselves when using a knife, or hurt their fingers when using a hammer. Tinkering School has been around for many years now, but nobody has ever suffered a serious injury in all those years. This is because there are strict health and safety regulations they must follow. The children always learn how to use the tools safely and they must wear the right clothing and protection at all times.

Gever Tulley's ideas have worked very well. A lot of children have gone to his summer schools over the years. In 2011, Gever Tulley and a colleague decided to create a 'real' school, called Brightworks, in San Francisco. The school is

very small – it only has 20 students aged 6 to 13. Brightworks is based on the same principles as Tinkering School.

Since it started, Brightworks has been written about a lot. Most of those articles have been very positive. They have praised the quality of the school. They have found the children are more motivated than at many other schools. But since the beginning of the school there have also been critical voices. Some people have said that children are not learning enough at Brightworks. They feel that students and teachers are just 'playing around' all the time.

The students at Brightworks seem to love their school. We spoke to 12-year-old Tina Cooper. She has been a student at the school since last October. 'Since I started here, I've never sat in a 'normal' class with a teacher,' she told us. 'But it's been a very exciting experience. I've worked hard at my new school for eight months now, and there hasn't been one single moment when I found it boring. Before, I was bored quite often.'

THiNK VALUES

Learning for life

1 Read the statements. Tick (✓) the things that you think kids are likely to learn at Tinkering School and Brightworks.

- [ ] Everyone is different and that's a good thing.
- [ ] Teamwork is important to achieve things in life.
- [ ] When you use a tool you have to be careful.
- [ ] It is important to be friendly and help others.
- [ ] It is very important in life to eat healthy food.
- [ ] Mistakes are important. We learn from them.

2 SPEAKING Compare your ideas with a partner.

I think they learn how to be careful with tools.   *Why?*

The text says there are strict health and safety regulations.   *Yes, I agree with you.*

3 SPEAKING Discuss these questions.

1 Which of the things from the list above do you think are important to learn?
2 What would you add to your personal list of 'Important things to learn'?

GRAMMAR
Present perfect with *for* and *since*

1 Look back at the article on page 21. <u>Underline</u> all the sentences in the present perfect.

2 Complete the sentences below with *for* and *since*. Then complete the rules.

1 Children have made fantastic things _____ the school started.
2 Tinkering School has been around _____ many years now.

> **RULE:** In the present perfect, we use
> - ¹_____ to talk about a period of time.
> - ²_____ to refer to the point in time when an action started.

3 When do we use *for* and when do we use *since*? Complete the chart with the words and phrases in the list.

a month | ~~last summer~~ | your birthday | yesterday
a year | 2014 | I phoned you | a long time
many years | days | Friday | an hour

for   *a month*   _____   _____
       _____   _____

since *last summer*   _____   _____
       _____   _____

4 Complete the sentences. Use the present perfect form of the verbs and *for* or *since*.

1 I _____ (be) at my new school _____ last December.
2 Hilary _____ (not see) Michael _____ several weeks.
3 They _____ (not write) an email or _____ (phone) us _____ three months.
4 He _____ (live) in this town _____ a long time.
5 I _____ (have) this camera _____ I was 10.

5 Write sentences using the present perfect with *for* or *since*.

0 Rebecca doesn't live in Italy now. (three years)
   Rebecca hasn't lived in Italy for three years.
1 They are in the youth club. (three hours)
2 Joanne and I are good friends. (primary school)
3 She plays in the volleyball team. (two months)
4 I ought to see a doctor. I am sick. (a week)
5 I don't hear a lot from Sandra. (last October)

> Workbook page 18

VOCABULARY
School subjects

1 🔊 1.15 Match the school subjects in the list with the photos. Write 1–12 in the boxes. Then listen and check.

1 Science (Physics, Biology and Chemistry)
2 Music | 3 Art Education | 4 Drama
5 Design and Technology | 6 Geography
7 English | 8 PE (Physical Education)
9 ICT (Information and Communication Technology)
10 Maths | 11 History | 12 Spanish

2 **SPEAKING** Answer the questions. Take notes. Then compare your answers with a partner.

1 Which are your favourite subjects? Which don't you like? Why?
2 Which of the subjects are you studying this year?
3 How long have you studied each subject?

> Workbook page 20

2 THE WAYS WE LEARN

LISTENING

1 Work in pairs. Match the activities with the photos.

1 make a fire | 2 spend a night outdoors | 3 climb a tree | 4 drive a car | 5 spend an hour blindfolded

2 **SPEAKING** Which of these things have you done? Tell your partner.

3 🔊 1.16 Listen to David talking about a book his father has just read. Which of the activities in Exercise 1 do they talk about?

4 🔊 1.16 Listen again. Mark the sentences T (true) or F (false).

1 David is babysitting his little brother. ___
2 David thinks the book his father read is nonsense. ___
3 The book says children should spend an hour blindfolded alone. ___
4 David is not sure his dad will let Nick drive a car. ___
5 Nick drove the car straight into a tree. ___
6 David thinks Nick will enjoy showing that he can make a fire. ___

FUNCTIONS
Asking and giving / refusing permission

1 Put the dialogues into the correct order. Write the numbers 1–4.

	DAD	Yes?
	DAD	I'm afraid I need it myself right now.
	NICK	Will you let me use your laptop?
	NICK	Dad?

	ANNIE	Can I watch the football match tonight?
	ANNIE	Can I ask you something, Mum?
	MUM	Yes, of course you can.
	MUM	Go ahead.

2 Mark the sentences AP (asking permission), GP (giving permission) or RP (refusing permission).

1 Will you let me use your camera? ___
   Yeah, sure. Of course I will. ___
2 Can I borrow your bike? ___
   No, sorry. I need it. ___
3 Can I use your laptop? ___
   Yes, you can, but I want it back tomorrow.
   ___
4 Is it OK if I borrow this necklace? ___
   Yeah, but be really careful with it, OK?
   ___

3 **ROLE PLAY** Work in pairs. Act out short conversations. Ask each other for permission. You can use the ideas here or come up with your own.

use his/her tablet | come with him/her
borrow £20 | copy his/her homework
get some help with homework

23

READING

1 Look at this picture. Think about the questions and compare your answers with a partner.

1 What does the picture show?
2 Where in the picture is the brain?
3 What does the brain do?

Learning is brain change

(1) Everybody has a brain, but not many people know how the brain works. Some people believe that the brain is like the hard disk of a computer. We use it to store files – images, language (words, texts, sounds) and other data. Others compare the brain to a huge container or cupboard with lots of little drawers, shelves and boxes in it. We put information into these boxes and hope to find it again later.

(2) The brain is not a computer disk, and it isn't a container. Look at the picture here. It looks a bit like weeds in a garden, doesn't it? The picture actually shows a child's neocortex – a part of the brain. You can guess what happens – more 'weeds' grow as the child gets older. Scientists call these neuronal networks. The networks grow around our neurons, or nerve cells. What makes them grow? Learning! 'Learning is brain change,' says Professor James Zull from Case Western University in Cleveland, Ohio, USA. 'Without learning, nothing changes in the brain. For every new word you learn in your English lesson, every puzzle you solve in maths, every new song you learn to sing, a neuronal network grows in your brain and the brain changes.'

(3) The more neuronal networks we grow, the better we can think and the better we remember. You may wonder if there is anything you can do to make the networks in your brain grow better. Professor Zull says yes, there is. He says that brain change is strongest when a) you are interested in and like what you are learning, b) you are in control of what you learn and c) you get challenging tasks that make you think hard and concentrate. Understanding a challenging task makes you feel good and develops your brain!

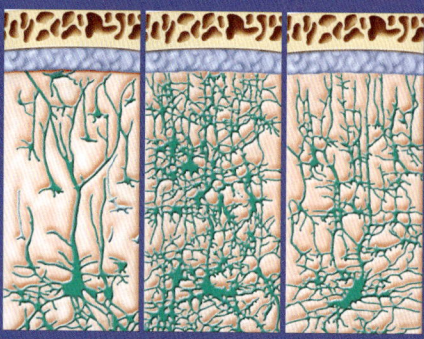

Neuronal networks at 9 months, 2 years and 4 years of age

2 Match the words with the meanings. Write the numbers 1–5. Then read the text to check your answers.

1 to store | 2 a container | 3 a weed
4 a nerve cell | 5 ~~to concentrate~~

a   to think very carefully about what you are doing   5
b   to keep things for use in the future
c   a wild plant that grows in a garden
d   it carries information between the brain and the body
e   an object used to carry or store things

3 Read the text again. Mark the sentences T (true) or F (false).

1 The text compares the brain to weeds. ___
2 The brain is a system of neuronal networks that can change. ___
3 Whenever we learn anything, a change happens in our brain. ___
4 We can't really make our brain stronger. ___
5 Being able to do difficult tasks is good for the brain. ___

TRAIN TO THiNK

Learning about texts

1 Choose the best description of this text.

A   an adventure story to entertain the reader.
B   an ad to sell the reader something.
C   a magazine article to give the reader information.
D   a letter to persuade the reader to do something.

2 Choose the title that best sums up the content of each paragraph. There is one extra title.

A   The brain – a fantastic computer ___
B   What people believe about the brain ___
C   How to make your brain stronger ___
D   Our brain is a growing system ___

2 THE WAYS WE LEARN

GRAMMAR
a, *an*, *the* or no article

1 Look at the sentences from a magazine article. Underline *a*, *an*, *the* and the nouns these articles are with. Then go through the sentences again and circle the nouns with no article. Finally complete the rule with *a*, *an*, *the*, – (no article).

> Food is important for your body. But did you know that the food you eat is important for your brain, too? Here is an example: sugar. Sugar tastes good. But the sugar from sweets can create problems. Your concentration and your memory get worse. What can we learn from the example here? It's better to eat an orange or a banana than to eat chocolate, because that's good for your brain and for your body.

> **RULE:** We use
> - _____ or _____ + a singular countable noun when the listener/reader doesn't know exactly which thing we are talking about.
>   *You can have **an apple** or **a banana**.*
>   *We've got **a new car**.*
> - _____ + noun when it is clear which thing(s) or person/people we are talking about.
>   ***The apples in this pie** are from our garden.*
>   ***The bananas that I bought** yesterday are horrible.*
> - _____ + plural countable noun or + uncountable noun, when we are talking about things in general.
>   ***Bananas** are sweeter than **apples**. **Chocolate** isn't good for you.*

2 Complete each sentence with *a*, *an*, *the* or – (no article).

0 She is __a__ good student.
1 She eats a lot of _____ fruit and _____ vegetables.
2 _____ book that you gave me was really good.
3 I have _____ idea. Let's watch _____ new Beyoncé video.
4 I never drink _____ coffee – I hate it.
5 I like lots of sports, but _____ sport I like most is _____ tennis.

3 Complete the text with *a*, *an*, *the* or –.

⁰ — People need to drink. Of course ¹_____ orange juice and ²_____ apple juice are very popular, but they are not always ³_____ good choice. ⁴_____ orange juice has got a lot of sugar in it, so don't drink too much of it. The best drink for your brain is ⁵_____ water. ⁶_____ glass of water is the best drink you can get, but ⁷_____ water that you drink needs to be fresh and clean.

Workbook page 19

VOCABULARY
Verbs about thinking

1 Use a dictionary to make sure you know the meaning of these words.

to concentrate on | to remember | to think
to imagine | to wonder | to believe
to guess | to recognise | to realise
to suppose

2 Choose the correct words.

1 The task was very difficult. I had to *remember* / *think* for a long time.
2 Come on, don't be silly. I don't *believe* / *realise* in ghosts!
3 Can you *imagine* / *concentrate* how great it must be to live at the beach?
4 When the teacher asked the question a different way, I *supposed* / *realised* that I knew the answer!
5 Did they really say they are moving to New York? I don't *suppose* / *believe* it!
6 I have not seen her for six years. I don't think I would *realise* / *recognise* her.
7 I have no idea what the answer is. I'll just have to *imagine* / *guess*.
8 I was so tired that I found it hard to *think* / *concentrate on* the test.
9 Have you ever *wondered* / *supposed* why I haven't phoned you for months?
10 If we want to get there faster, I *wonder* / *suppose* we should take a taxi.

Pronunciation
Word stress
Go to page 120.

3 **SPEAKING** Work in pairs. Ask and answer questions.

1 Are there any places where you can think really well or not well at all?
2 Does music help you to concentrate or make it difficult for you to concentrate? Does it matter what kind of music it is?
3 In what situations can you imagine things really well? Do you find it difficult to use your imagination sometimes?
4 Do you find it difficult to remember things sometimes? What sort of things?
5 Do you believe in life on other planets? What do you suppose the people there look like?

Workbook page 20

Culture

A day in the life of …

1 🔊 1.19 Look at the photos. What do you think a typical day for a student at each of these three schools is like? Read and listen to check.

1 Alexander, student at a Dance Academy in Moscow, Russia

I've been at this dance Academy for three years. This is a typical day for me:

I get up around eight o'clock, have a quick breakfast, do my hair, and get into my dance clothes. I arrive at the school around 8.45, just in time for the warm-up before class.

My first class, classical ballet, starts at 9.00 and finishes at 10.30. I then have a 20-minute break. I eat a banana on the way to another building. As soon as I arrive there, my modern dance class starts. It runs until 12.15. Then I have a 45-minute lunch break. In the afternoon it's classical ballet again, then gymnastics to strengthen the muscles. I get home around seven, and I'm usually very tired.

On Saturdays, I only have a one-and-a-half-hour ballet class, and on Sundays I'm free.

2 Ethan, college basketball player from Chicago, USA

My day starts at 8 am with the weight training program. We do a ten-minute warm-up, and then it's hard work for 50 minutes.

At nine o'clock my classes start. When we have an away match, we can't do so much school work. When we are back at school, we have to work harder than the others. But I'm not complaining – I've been in the team for more than a year now, and it's cool.

I have a break between 1.00 and 2.30. I try to take only 30 minutes for lunch and the rest I use for studying. The afternoon is full of classes and practice.

At night I have to watch videos of games, I have to read books about basketball and study for my exams, too. When I finally go to bed – often nearly midnight – I'm completely exhausted!

3 Ella, drama student from Sydney, Australia

6.45: I'm not good at getting up early. Three alarm clocks – at 6.30, 6.40 and 6.50.

8.00: Voice training. Important for an actor.

8.45: Gymnastics – I like it. It helps me concentrate better and makes me feel good.

9.30: Singing and dance workshop. It's hard work, but it gives me energy. Music and rhythm. Love it!

11.00: First break – drink, drink, drink – water, of course. No drinks with sugar in them. Makes the body and the mind tired.

11.15: Performance workshop. Hard work. Our teachers are fantastic, but they tell you when you make mistakes!

12.30: Lunch break – I eat nuts and fruit, or a salad at one of the cafés nearby. I never eat carbohydrates, you know, pasta or other heavy stuff.

2.00: A lecture about acting, for example, how to move on the stage, what to do with your hands, etc. Not always easy to concentrate after lunch.

3.30: Short break. I try not to fall asleep. The day has been very tiring!

3.45: Voice training workshop, dance and singing.

6.00: Evening rehearsal. We practise for a performance at the end of term. We're doing a musical this term. Hard work and great fun.

9.00: I go home.

10.00: Zzzz!

2 THE WAYS WE LEARN

2 Read the article again. Complete the sentences with *Alexander*, *Ethan* or *Ella*.

1 _____ often studies for many hours at night.
2 _____ knows very well what to eat and what to drink.
3 _____'s life is more relaxed at weekends.
4 _____ is free in the evenings.
5 _____ learns about body language.
6 _____ accepts that other students sometimes have to work less.

3 VOCABULARY Read the article again. Find words or phrases with the following meaning.

1 make my hair look good (story 1) *do my hair*
2 gentle exercises you do before doing a sport to prepare your body (story 1) _____
3 a very traditional type of dancing (story 1) _____
4 to make something stronger (story 1) _____
5 exercise that makes the muscles stronger (story 2) _____
6 a match that a team plays at the sports ground of the other team (story 2) _____
7 almost midnight (story 2) _____
8 extremely tired (story 2) _____
9 a formal talk given to a group of students (story 3) _____
10 food such as bread, potatoes or rice (story 3) _____
11 a type of lesson where you learn something practical (story 3) _____
12 the action of entertaining other people by dancing, singing, etc. (story 3) _____

WRITING
An email describing your school routine

1 Read this email from your friend in Cambridge. Then answer the questions.

1 How does Kylie feel about her new class?
2 What does Kylie think of Luca and why?
3 Does Kylie think you've gozvt less school work than her?
4 How does her work for school compare to last year?
5 What subject does she get a lot of homework for, and how does she feel about it?

2 Underline sentences in the email where Kylie writes about these things. What tense does she use in the sentences you underlined? Why does she use it?

a asks how you feel about your new school
b talks about Luca's father
c compares school this year to last year
d talks about the amount of homework this year

3 Put the words in the right order. Write the sentences. What tense are they in and why?

1 new / too / class / kid / There's / a / my / in
2 a week / at / four times / come home / 5.30 / I
3 love / projects / I / class / But / the / do / this / in / we

4 Match the four paragraphs of Kylie's email with the content.

Paragraph 1   a   Kylie's new class
Paragraph 2   b   a request to write soon
Paragraph 3   c   an introduction
Paragraph 4   d   work this year compared to last

5 Read Kylie's email again. Make notes with your own ideas on how:

a to answer the question in her introduction
b to describe your new class (new school? classmates?)
c to compare your work this year to last year's
d to say how you feel about your subjects (any subjects you particularly like/don't like? Why?)
e you could finish your email (What do you want to know from Kylie?)

6 Write an email to Kylie (about 200 words). Look at your notes from Exercise 5 and make sure you include all your ideas. Make sure you use the present continuous when necessary.

Hi there!

I hope this finds you well. I haven't heard from you since the beginning of the holidays. Are you enjoying your new school?

I am, big time! I'm in a class with all my friends again – Emily, Kate, James and all the others. There's a new kid in my class too. His name's Luca and he's from Bologna in Italy. His father is working in the UK for a year, and the whole family have come over. He's cool. We have lots of fun together.

But of course, it's not all fun. We've got important exams this year so there's a lot of work to do. I'm spending more time at school than last year, and I come home at 5.30 four times a week. We're also getting a lot more homework, especially for Technology and Design. But I love the projects we do in this class!

Well, I guess it's not so different for you. If you've got a bit of time, please let me know how things are going. I'd really like to know what life at school is like for you. And remember, please, you've got a friend in Cambridge who would really like to get mail from you more often!

Write soon!

Kylie

CAMBRIDGE ENGLISH: Preliminary

THiNK EXAMS

READING
Part 3: True/false

1 Look at the sentences. Read the text below to decide if each sentence is correct or incorrect. If it is correct, tick (✓) the box under A. If it is incorrect, tick (✓) the box under B.

A   B

1 The Tan-y-Bryn Outdoor Adventure Centre gets visitors from many different European countries.
2 Children learn about the countryside from books there.
3 The Centre is only open to school children.
4 The Centre offers three meals a day.
5 No one has been badly hurt during activities at the Centre.
6 The Centre will send people to talk to your family if you are interested in going.

Tan-y-Bryn Outdoor Adventure Centre

Since opening our doors in 1975, Tan-y-Bryn Outdoor Centre has welcomed thousands of young people from all over the UK to enjoy fun, education and adventure in the beautiful Welsh countryside. Whether they are climbing on the slopes of Mount Snowdon, snorkelling in the Menai Straits or birdwatching in the woodlands, our visitors enjoy hands-on experiences they will never forget.

For school groups, youth clubs and families we offer comfortable accommodation for up to 50 children and 10 adults. We also provide a full breakfast, lunch and dinner to make sure no one goes hungry. Safety is a top priority – there has never been a serious accident at the Centre.

Where are we? On the island of Anglesey in North Wales. By car, take the A4080 and follow the signs for Dwyran and then the Centre.

What do we offer? Outdoor activities – mountain biking, trail walking, geocaching, canoeing – as well as sports – everything from archery to tennis and football.

How do I find out more? Email us. For large bookings, a representative can visit your school or youth club to answer questions.

LISTENING
Part 1: Multiple choice

2 🔊 1.20 For each question, there are three pictures and a short recording. Choose the correct picture and put a tick (✓) in the box below it.

1 What did Sally buy at the shops?

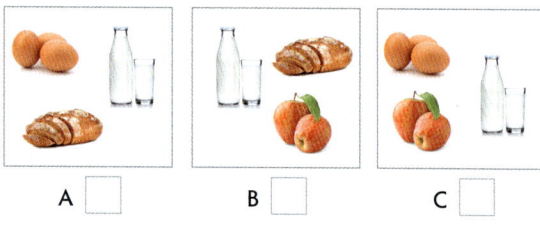

A   B   C

2 What time is it?

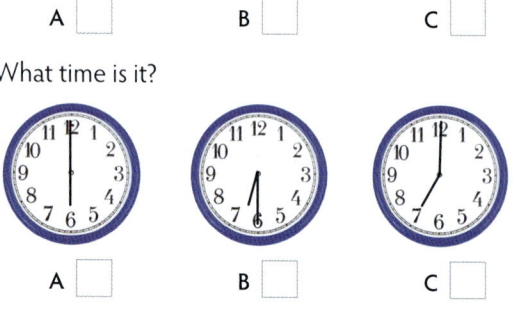

A   B   C

3 How did Brian get to work?

A   B    C

4 Which lesson did Fred enjoy most?

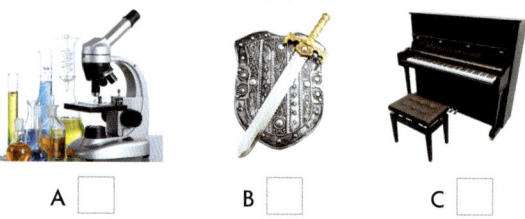

A   B   C

5 When is Tom's brother's birthday?

A   B    C

TEST YOURSELF

UNITS 1 & 2

VOCABULARY

1 Complete the sentences with the words in the list. There are two extra words.

signed | wrote | brave | guess | recognise | creative
missed | won | wonder | believe | realise | active

1 It was my first competition, and I _____ it!
2 My granddad's quite old, but he's still very _____ – he's always doing things!
3 When his daughter was born, he _____ a song about her.
4 I didn't like the birthday cards in the shop, so I decided to be _____ and make one.
5 It's strange that Maggie isn't here. I _____ where she is.
6 It's eleven o'clock! Wow! I didn't _____ it was so late.
7 I didn't know the answer, so I had to _____ .
8 She didn't run away when the dog was running towards her – she was very _____ .
9 I'm sure he saw me, but he didn't say hello. Maybe he didn't _____ me.
10 I enjoyed my year in the USA, but I really _____ my family.

/10

GRAMMAR

2 Complete the sentences with the words in the list. You need to write the correct form of the verbs.

not see (x2) | not open (x2) | bus | the bus

1 My parents gave me my present this morning, but I _____ it yet.
2 I'm tired, I don't want to walk. Let's go by _____ .
3 She was at the party? Really? I _____ her there.
4 There was a sign on the door that said 'No entry!', so I _____ it.
5 There's a new film at the cinema, but I _____ it yet.
6 We were late because _____ arrived 30 minutes late.

3 Find and correct the mistake in each sentence.

1 Can I have a glass of a water, please?
2 I've travelled to already more than ten countries.
3 We've lived here since three years.
4 I've gone to a party last night.
5 This is my bicycle. I had it for two years.
6 It's important to eat a lot of the fruit if you want to be healthy.

/12

FUNCTIONAL LANGUAGE

4 Write the missing words. Choose from the words in the list.

afraid | Can | definitely | go | idea | Let's | OK | thinking

1 A _____ I use your dictionary, please?
  B Sorry, I'm _____ I'm using it right now.
2 A _____ watch a film on DVD tonight.
  B That's a great _____ !
3 A I'm _____ about doing a walk for charity. What do you think?
  B Yes, you should _____ do it.
4 A Is it _____ if I use your computer?
  B Yes, of course, _____ ahead.

/8

MY SCORE /30

22 – 30
10 – 21
0 – 9

29

3 THAT'S ENTERTAINMENT

OBJECTIVES

FUNCTIONS: comparing things and actions; asking for and offering help
GRAMMAR: comparative and superlative adjectives (review); (not) as … as; making a comparison stronger or weaker; adverbs
VOCABULARY: types of films; types of TV programmes; expressions with *get*

READING

1 Match the words and pictures. Write 1–6 in the boxes.

   1 a video game | 2 a concert | 3 a film
   4 a play | 5 a sports event | 6 a TV programme

2 **SPEAKING** Which of these kinds of entertainment do you like? Tell your partner.

3 **SPEAKING** Work in small groups. Talk about the things in Exercise 1. Say why people like or don't like them. Use the words in the list to help you.

   relaxing | interesting | fun | expensive
   crowds | friends | enjoyable

   I think people enjoy watching a film because it is relaxing.

4 Look at the pictures and the title of the article on the next page. What do you think the article is about?

   1 the high price of horror films
   2 the salaries of famous film actors
   3 a film that was made very cheaply

5 🔊 1.21 Read and listen to the article and check your ideas.

6 Read the article again. Find:

   1 two examples of very expensive films.
   2 two reasons why it is possible to say that *Monsters* was successful.
   3 four reasons why *Monsters* wasn't expensive to make.
   4 the amount of time Gareth Edwards worked on the film after filming.

A

B

C

D

E

F

3 THAT'S ENTERTAINMENT

Big movies
on a small budget

Do you need millions of dollars to make a movie? No. Do you need millions of dollars to make a *successful* movie? Most people would answer 'Yes' to that question. But would they be right?

We're used to hearing about really expensive Hollywood films. The 1997 Oscar-winner *Titanic* cost $200 million to make, and more recently, *Spider Man 3*, one of the most successful films of 2007, had a budget of more than $250 million.

To be successful, however, a film doesn't need to be as expensive as the big Hollywood blockbusters. An example of this is the 2010 movie *Monsters*, which cost less than half a million dollars to make. *Monsters* is set in Mexico and is the story of two people trying to escape from aliens and get back to the USA. The film won several awards and got very good reviews from many film critics – for example, the website Moviefone put *Monsters* at number 3 in its list of the best sci-fi films for 2010.

How did they make the film so cheaply? First of all, it only took three weeks to film, and the film crew was just seven people in a van. Secondly, the man who made the film, Gareth Edwards, decided to film it with digital video, which is cheaper than the usual 35mm film. (The film equipment cost only $15,000 altogether.) There is also the fact that they used real locations, not a studio. And the cast of the film were Edwards himself and two friends of his – all the extras in the film were people who were just there, and they weren't paid.

Most importantly, Edwards did most of the production work himself. He spent eight months editing *Monsters* and then five months creating the special effects. And he did it all at home on his computer, using non-professional software. The amazing thing is that the final film looks nearly as professional as big, fancy Hollywood productions.

Not everybody liked *Monsters*, of course. One person said: 'That's 90 minutes of my life that I'll never get back.' But overall, it was very well received. And at least it wasn't expensive to make.

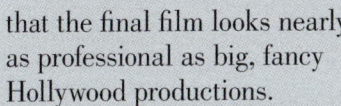

Spending wisely

1 **Read the sentences. How much do you agree with each one? Write a number: 1 (I agree) or 2 (I'm not sure) or 3 (I don't agree).**

   1 If something is expensive, you can be sure it's really good. ☐
   2 Expensive things are usually not worth the money. ☐
   3 You can find really good things that don't cost a lot of money. ☐
   4 It doesn't matter how much something costs. ☐
   5 It's crazy to like something just because it is expensive. ☐

2 **Compare your ideas in the class.**

> I don't agree with number one. Some expensive things aren't good.

> Do you think so? I agree with it. If you buy cheap things, they're usually not good.

31

GRAMMAR
Comparative and superlative adjectives (review)

1 Complete these sentences about the article on page 31 with the correct form of the words in the list. Then complete the rules.

good | cheap | boring | expensive

1 They used digital video because it's _____ than 35mm film.
2 Moviefone thought *Monsters* was one of the _____ films of the year.
3 Most Hollywood films are _____ than *Monsters*.
4 One person thought *Monsters* was the _____ film ever.

(not) as … as comparatives

2 Look at the examples of (*not*) *as … as* to compare things. Answer the questions. Then complete the rule.

Extras aren't as expensive as actors.
Monsters looks as professional as Hollywood films.

1 Who are more expensive: extras or actors?
2 Do Hollywood films look more professional than *Monsters*?

RULE: When we want to say that two things are (not) the same, we can use (*not*) _____ + adjective + _____ .

3 Complete each sentence with ideas of your own.
1 Football isn't as exciting as *skiing* .
2 Football is more exciting than *golf* .
3 Potatoes are healthier than _____ .
4 Potatoes aren't as healthy as _____ .
5 English is easier than _____ .
6 English isn't as easy as _____ .
7 Watching TV isn't as good as _____ .
8 Watching TV is better than _____ .

4 Complete the second sentence so it has the same meaning as the first. Use the word in brackets.

0 Ben's sister is younger than him. (old)
Ben's sister *isn't as old as* him.
1 Travelling by train is faster than travelling by bus. (slow)
Travelling by train _____ travelling by bus.
2 Tom is 1.65. Sue is 1.65, too. (tall)
Tom _____ Sue.
3 Dogs are noisier than cats. (quiet)
Dogs _____ cats.
4 This mobile phone costs €225. And the bicycle costs €225, too. (expensive)
The mobile phone _____ the bicycle.
5 Jo thinks geography is easier than history. (difficult)
Jo thinks geography _____ history.
6 My room is tidier than yours. (untidy)
My room _____ yours.

Pronunciation
Words ending in /ə/
Go to page 120.

Workbook page 28

VOCABULARY
Types of films

Workbook page 31

1 Write the types of films in the list under the pictures.

action film | animated film | documentary
comedy | horror film | romantic comedy (rom com)
science fiction (sci-fi) | thriller

2 **SPEAKING** Can you think of an example of each kind of film? Are there any films which are more than one kind?

Madagascar is an animated film and it's a comedy, too.

1 _____

2 _____

3 _____

4 _____

5 _____

6 _____

7 _____

8 _____

3 THAT'S ENTERTAINMENT

LISTENING

1 **1.24** Listen to Part 1 of an interview. Why is Sandra Allen a guest on the radio show?

   1 She won a prize for acting.
   2 She won a prize for making a film.
   3 She made a film and hopes to win a prize.

2 **1.25** Listen to Part 2 of the interview. Choose the correct answers.

   1 She chose one of the actors for her film because
      A he wanted to act at school.
      B he had useful things for making the film.
      C he was in the football team.

   2 When she wrote the script for the film, Sandra
      A tried to make it shorter.
      B included a lot of different people and places.
      C asked a friend to improve it.

   3 Sandra says that the most important thing for making a film is
      A having special equipment.
      B seeing the final film in your head.
      C editing the film to make it shorter.

3 **1.26** Listen to Part 3, in which Sandra says what her film is about. Complete the text.

It starts in a school classroom – I used my school of course, and ¹_____ sitting around. And the two actors are sitting talking ²_____ and they start saying how everything is really boring, you know? And another guy is watching them and ³_____, and then he gets up and walks down a corridor into ⁴_____. And in there, we see him pull a big, black handle – and everything goes into ⁵_____ ! And everyone at the school is surprised and ⁶_____ but they don't know what's happened. So the film is about how everyone really, really wants to get the colour ⁷_____. In the end, everything does go ⁸_____. And the couple in the film are in the same place, but now they see it ⁹_____.

GRAMMAR
Making a comparison stronger or weaker

1 Read the sentences. Circle the phrase that has a different meaning from the other two. Then complete the rules.

   0 I think independent movies are *a lot* / *much* / *(a little)* more interesting.
   1 I had to make it *a little* / *a lot* / *a bit* shorter.
   2 The final script was *a little* / *much* / *far* better than the first version.

   RULE: Use _____ / _____ / *far* to make a comparative stronger.
   Use *a bit* / _____ to make a comparative weaker.

2 Rewrite these sentences using the words in brackets.

   0 Snakes are more dangerous than bears. (a lot)
      Snakes are a lot more dangerous than bears.
   1 My brother is taller than me. (a bit)
   2 My new phone's better than the old one. (far)
   3 Her nails are longer than yours. (a little)
   4 The film's more exciting than the book. (much)

3 Write sentences comparing these things. Use *much* / *far* / *a lot*, or *a bit* / *a little*.

   1 watching TV / reading a book (interesting / easy)
      I think watching TV is a lot more interesting than reading a book – and it's far easier, too.
   2 a mobile phone / an MP4 player (useful / expensive)
   3 gorillas / snakes (dangerous / beautiful)
   4 English / Art (difficult / interesting)
   5 my country / USA (big / beautiful)

   ➤ Workbook page 29

THiNK SELF-ESTEEM

The film of my life

1 Write some ideas for a film script based on your life. Think about these things as you write.

   1 How old are you at the beginning of the film?
   2 Which other people will be in the film with you?
   3 What will be the funniest scene in the film?
   4 How will you end the film?

2 **SPEAKING** Work in pairs. Talk about your films.

READING

1 Read the TV listings. Write the type of programme on each channel.

CHANNEL 1	CHANNEL 2	CHANNEL 3	CHANNEL 4	CHANNEL 5
8.00 pm **Down Our Street**	**8.00 pm** **Double Your Money**	**8.00 pm** **19th-century House**	**8.00 pm** **The News**	**8.00 pm** **The Jordan Baker Show**
Your favourite soap continues with Jim and Amanda having an argument, while Alex still can't find a job. Tom has asked Joanna to marry him but she's got some doubts, and then her friend Tracey tells her a few things about Tom that she didn't know!	Jason Oates is the host of the popular game show where the contestants can win £10,000 – and then double it! There are questions on all kinds of topics to test everyone's general knowledge. Which of tonight's players will get the chance to double their money?	Our reality show continues, now with only eight of the twelve contestants, all living in a house from 200 years ago. It isn't easy living with no electricity, no heating and no 21st-century technology at all. And it's even more difficult with cameras on you 24 hours a day. (Don't forget to have your phone ready to vote.)	All the news and sport from around the world. With Michael Webster.	Jordan Baker presents her completely new chat show. She talks to great celebrity guests and asks them the questions that everyone wants to know the answers to. Tonight, athletics star Sally Malone.
soap opera				

2 Read the programme descriptions again. Answer the questions.
1. Which two programmes have contestants?
2. Which three programmes have presenters?
3. Which programme has actors in it?
4. Which programme asks viewers to participate?

3 **PET** Read these tweets. Match the tweets with the programmes.

Adam Windsor @adamgwindsor — 4m
They were really bad this week. I answered all the questions easily. I did better than them! All that money and nobody won it! #DYM

Jenny Kool @kooljenny — 15m
Ha ha She needs to think carefully before she says Yes. More carefully than her sister before she got married. Reckon she should say No! lol
#joannathinkaboutit

Paul @earlybird2015 — 17m
Can't understand what Gavin says when he speaks. He should speak more clearly. Going to vote him off. Hope Jackie wins lol!
#gojackiego

4 **SPEAKING** Work in groups. Choose one of the programmes to watch tonight. Tell the others why you chose it.

I'm going to watch Double Your Money because I really like quiz shows. You can learn things, and it's fun to watch the contestants – especially when they get the answers wrong!

GRAMMAR
Adverbs and comparative adverbs

1 Look at the sentences from the TV listings. Complete them with the words in the list.

popular | easy | easily | carefully

1. It isn't _____ living without electricity.
2. I answered the questions _____ .
3. She needs to think _____ .
4. He's the host of a _____ game show.

3 THAT'S ENTERTAINMENT

2 Circle the adverbs in the previous exercise. Then complete the rules with *adjective* and *adverb*.

RULES:
- Use an _____ to talk about a noun:
  He's a *slow runner*.
- Use an _____ to talk about a verb:
  He *runs slowly*.

We usually form an _____ by adding *-ly* (or *-ily*) to the _____ , but some adverbs are irregular: *fast → fast, good → well*.

3 Write the adverbs.

0 quick *quickly*
1 careful _____
2 clever _____
3 clear _____
4 good _____
5 bad _____
6 easy _____
7 fast _____

4 Look at the examples of comparative adverbs from the tweets on page 34. Then complete the rules.

1 She should think **more carefully** than her sister did.
2 He should speak **more clearly**.
3 I answered the questions **better** than them.

RULE: To form the comparative of most regular adverbs, add the word _____ before the adverb.

If an adverb has one syllable, make the comparative by adding *-er*: *soon → sooner, hard → harder, fast → faster*.
- There are some irregular comparative adverbs: *badly → worse, well → better*.
- Notice that the comparative of *early* is written *earlier*.

5 Complete the sentences. Use the comparative adverb forms of the words in brackets.

0 Sue runs *faster* (fast) than me.
1 Graham writes _____ (clear) than me.
2 You need to do your homework _____ (careful) if you want to get good marks.
3 Sorry, I don't understand. Can you speak _____ (slow), please?
4 The party starts at ten o'clock, but you can come _____ (early) if you want to.
5 I only got 22% in the test, but you did even _____ (bad) than me!
6 Sandra always works _____ (hard) than the other kids.
7 Martina speaks English _____ (good) than I do.

> Workbook page 29

VOCABULARY
Types of TV programmes

1 Look at the different types of TV programmes. Can you think of an example for each one?

chat show — news — drama series — cartoon — game show — reality show — sitcom — soap (opera) — sports programme — talent show

2 SPEAKING Work in pairs. Ask and answer the questions.

1 What kind(s) of programmes do you really like?
2 What kind(s) of programmes do you really NOT like?
3 What programme on TV now do you always watch? Why?
4 What programme on TV now do you never watch? Why?
5 How do you watch TV programmes – on TV, on your phone, on a tablet …?

> Workbook page 31

WRITING
A paragraph

Write a paragraph about your TV habits.
- Use your answers to the questions in Vocabulary Exercise 2 to help you.
- Try to use grammar and vocabulary from the unit (comparative adjectives, words for TV programmes, etc.)

PHOTOSTORY: episode 2

Extras

1 Look at the photos and answer the questions.
Why does Megan want to be an extra in the film?
Why is Megan unhappy in the last photo?

2 🔊 1.27 Now read and listen to the photostory. Check your answers.

LUKE Guys, guys! Guess what!
OLIVIA They're going to make a film here.
LUKE Oh. Right. You've heard then?
RYAN We have. They're going to do some filming in the park. For a new sci-fi movie. And Megan's really excited.
MEGAN I really am. Gregory Harris is in the film. He's so cool. In fact, I think he's my favourite actor of all time!

LUKE Don't get too excited, Megan. You're not going to meet him. Or even see him, probably.
RYAN Don't be so sure, Luke. The thing is, they want extras for the film.
LUKE Extras?
MEGAN You know – the people who stand around and do things but don't say anything.
LUKE Oh, come on, Megan. Everybody knows what extras are.

MEGAN Oh, sorry. Anyway, they're going to choose people to be extras today. One o'clock at the Sports Centre in town. I'm definitely going. Imagine – me, in a film with Gregory Harris!
OLIVIA Ryan's going, and so am I. How about you, Luke?
LUKE OK, why not? One o'clock at the Sports Centre? Let's all meet there then.

RYAN That's odd. There's no one here.
OLIVIA Have a look at this, guys. The time was eleven o'clock, not one o'clock.
MEGAN Oh, no! I read it wrong. I saw eleven and thought it was one! Oh, how could I be so stupid?
LUKE Looks like you're not going to meet Gregory Harris after all, Megan.
MEGAN Oh, leave me alone, Luke!

3 THAT'S ENTERTAINMENT

DEVELOPING SPEAKING

3 Work in pairs. Discuss what happens next in the story. Write down your ideas.

We think Ryan goes to see the film director to try to help Megan.

4 ◼ EP2 Watch to find out how the story continues.

5 Mark the sentences T (true) or F (false).

1. Tony Gorman is from Britain. ___
2. He is the director of the film. ___
3. He buys a coffee for Megan. ___
4. Megan listens to Tony's phone call. ___
5. Megan recognises the second man who comes into the coffee shop. ___
6. She comes back to the park with an autographed photo of Gregory Harris. ___

PHRASES FOR FLUENCY

1 Find the expressions 1–6 in the story. Who says them? How do you say them in your language?

1. Guess what?
2. In fact, …
3. Come on, …
4. Have a look [at this]
5. Looks like …
6. … after all.

2 Complete the conversation. Use the expressions in Exercise 1.

JIM   Hi guys. [1]_____ ? I'm in the football team!
MIKE You're joking!
JIM   No, I'm not. [2]_____ at this. It's the team list.
MIKE But you're not a good player, Jim. [3]_____, you're terrible!
ALICE Oh, [4]_____, Mike! He's not so bad.
SUSIE That's right. And the school has picked him to play, so [5]_____ you're wrong, Mike.
MIKE Well, I guess so.
JIM   Yes. I'm good enough for the school team [6]_____!

WordWise
Expressions with *get*

1 Look at the sentences from the unit so far. Choose the correct meaning of *get* in each one.

1. They're trying to **get** back to the USA.
2. Can I **get** you another drink?
3. Who will **get** the chance to double their money?
4. Don't **get** too excited, Megan.

a become
b receive
c go, arrive
d bring, buy

2 Use a phrase from the list to complete each sentence.

get home | got bored | got there
get a drink | get angry | got better

1. The film was terrible – after 20 minutes, I _____ and fell asleep.
2. I was really late for school – when I _____, it was already ten o'clock!
3. There's still a long way to go. We won't _____ before midnight, I think.
4. He was ill for about a week, but then he _____, I'm happy to say.
5. It was just a joke. Please don't _____ with me!
6. If you want, we can _____ in that café in the town centre.

3 Match the questions and answers.

1. Let's go and get a drink. ☐
2. When do you get angry with people? ☐
3. Do you ever get bored watching TV? ☐
4. What time do you get to school? ☐
5. Do you ever get a cold? ☐

a When they say things I don't like.
b Usually about eight o'clock.
c OK. The shop over there sells water.
d Sometimes – in winter, usually.
e Only when it's a programme I don't like.

4 Now write *your* answers to questions 2–5 in Exercise 3.

▶ Workbook page 31

FUNCTIONS
Asking for and offering help

1 Look at two sentences from the video. Which one is asking for help? Which one is offering help?

1. Can I help you?
2. Could you help me with something?

2 Now look at these sentences. Are they asking or offering help?

1. Can you lend me a hand?
2. Do you need any help?
3. Have you got a few minutes?
4. Is everything OK?

3 **SPEAKING** Work in pairs. Use the questions in Exercises 1 and 2 to act out conversations in a shop, at home, at school and other places.

4 SOCIAL NETWORKING

OBJECTIVES

FUNCTIONS: giving advice
GRAMMAR: indefinite pronouns (*everyone, no one, someone,* etc.) *all / some / none / any of them; should(n't), had better, ought to*
VOCABULARY: IT terms; language for giving advice

READING

1 **SPEAKING** Work in pairs. Answer the questions.
   1 Which of these social networks do you know about?
   2 What do you think of them?
   3 Do you know about any other social networks?

2 **SPEAKING** Read these statements about using social networks. Which of them are true for you? Discuss them with a partner.
   1 I've got a Facebook account but hardly ever use it.
   2 I don't post many comments, but I like to read other people's posts.
   3 I constantly check for updates on social media.
   4 I sometimes post comments that I regret later.
   5 I know of a post that created a problem.

3 🔊 1.28 Read and listen to the article about online behaviour to decide if each sentence is correct or incorrect. If it's correct, mark it A. If it's incorrect, mark it B.
   1 James Miller did not think before he wrote a post and so he lost his job. ☐
   2 His boss apologised for giving James work that wasn't very interesting. ☐
   3 Cathy's birthday party ended in disaster because her parents went out that evening. ☐
   4 A study from last year shows a lot of teens had problems because of their behaviour on the web. ☐
   5 The writer of the article thinks that you can't make everybody happy with your posts. ☐
   6 He says that before writing a post you should think of reactions you might get. ☐
   7 He thinks that we need to be as friendly online as we are in real life. ☐
   8 He says that posting things when you're unhappy is a good way to feel better. ☐

4 Work in pairs. Correct the statements marked B.

4 SOCIAL NETWORKING

Think before you act online

Sometimes what we post on our favourite social networks can have consequences we didn't expect. One weekend, 20-year-old James Miller posted on his Facebook page that his job was 'soooo boring'. When he got to work on Monday his boss told him to clear his desk and get out. He gave him a letter, too. It said: 'After reading your comments on Facebook about our company, we understand you are not happy with your work. We think it is better for you to look for something that you will find more interesting.'

A few years ago, a girl's birthday party turned into a nightmare. Fifteen-year-old Cathy posted an invitation to her birthday party online. She posted her address, too. When her parents got back from the cinema that evening, they couldn't believe their eyes. There were 500 people at the party, and some of them were smashing windows, breaking potted plants and making a total mess of the house.

Most teens think they know everything about social media, and that things like this could never happen to them. A study shows that last year alone, more than three million young people worldwide got into trouble because of their online activities.

Here are some important tips. None of them can guarantee 100% Internet security, but all of them will help you to be safer online.

RULE 1: Share with care!
Not everyone will like what you write on Facebook or Twitter. Think before you post something. You can never completely control who sees your profile, your texts, your pictures, or your videos. Before clicking 'post', everyone should ask themselves two questions: 'How will I feel if my family or teachers see this?' and 'How might this post be bad for me in three, five or ten years from now?'

RULE 2: Be polite when you write!
Imagine someone is unfriendly in real life. You don't like it, right? Well, the same is true of online communication. Politeness matters, and anyone can be polite. No one likes it when you 'shout' in your messages. DON'T USE ALL CAPITALS!!!!!!!! If you feel angry or frustrated while you're writing a message, wait a bit. Read it again later and then send it.

RULE 3: Protect and respect!
Don't share your passwords with anyone. Don't post your home or email address online. Beware of 'cyberbullying' – don't forward rumours about other people, and don't say negative things about them. If you get messages like that or see them online, talk to an adult you know.

THiNK VALUES

Responsible online behaviour

1 Read the statements. Write them in two lists under *Do* and *Don't*.
- say bad things about other people online.
- talk to your teacher or another adult if you get bullied on social media.
- think carefully before you write a post about yourself or other people.
- write a post about someone when you are angry with them.
- write posts containing personal information about your family.
- think before you post a photo of yourself or someone else.

2 **SPEAKING** Work in pairs. Compare your lists with your partner. Think of at least two more statements for each list.

GRAMMAR
Indefinite pronouns (everyone, no one, someone etc.)

1 **Complete these sentences from the article on page 39. Underline other examples of indefinite pronouns in the article.**

1 Most teens think they know _____ about social media.
2 Think before you post _____ .
3 _____ likes it when you 'shout' in your messages.

2 **Complete the table. Use the article on page 39 to help you. Then complete the rule with** *some / any / no / every*.

everything	something	nothing	anything
everyone	1_____	2_____	3_____
everywhere	somewhere	nowhere	anywhere

> **RULE:** The words beginning with
> - _____ mean 'all' (people / things / places).
> - _____ mean that we don't know exactly which (person / thing / place).
> - _____ mean that we don't care or it doesn't matter which (person / thing / place).
> - _____ mean 'not any' (person / thing / place).

3 **Complete the sentences with words from the table in Exercise 2.**

1 Where's my pen? I've looked _____ , but I can't find it.
2 Using social media can be a real problem. _____ should know that.
3 The teacher asked a question, but _____ knew the answer.
4 _____ left a message for you at reception.
5 Ouch! There's _____ in my eye!
6 I've no idea where Sally is. She could be _____ .
7 Do you want a place to relax on your holiday? There's _____ better than here!
8 It's so noisy. Let's go _____ quieter.

4 **Complete the sentences so that they are true for you.**

1 Everyone knows that I …
2 For my next holiday I'd like to go somewhere …
3 I don't like eating anything that has got … in it.
4 I think anyone can learn to …

▶ Workbook page 36

VOCABULARY
IT terms

1 **Match the phrases with the definitions. Write the numbers 1–10.**

1 to key in your password
2 to install a programme
3 to attach a file │ 4 to have network coverage
5 to upload a photo │ 6 to delete a message
7 ~~to open an attachment~~ │ 8 to buy an app
9 to activate flight mode
10 to download a file

a to click on the icon of a file that comes with an email — **7**
b to have a signal that lets you make phone calls, etc. ☐
c to add a separate element (e.g. a photo, a document, a video) to an email ☐
d to make an image available on the Internet ☐
e to pay for a programme for your mobile or tablet ☐
f to type a secret word that gives you access to a computer ☐
g to put a programme on a computer ☐
h to switch on a function on your mobile or tablet so you can't go online ☐
i to remove a piece of text so it cannot be seen any more ☐
j to copy information or a programme from the Internet onto your computer hard disk ☐

2 **SPEAKING** Work in pairs. Ask and answer the questions.

1 How easy or difficult is it for you to go online?
2 How often do you post something on social media?
3 What kind of things do you usually post?
4 What ways do you know of keeping passwords secure but remembering them?

3 **Draw mind maps for these verbs.**

▶ Workbook page 38

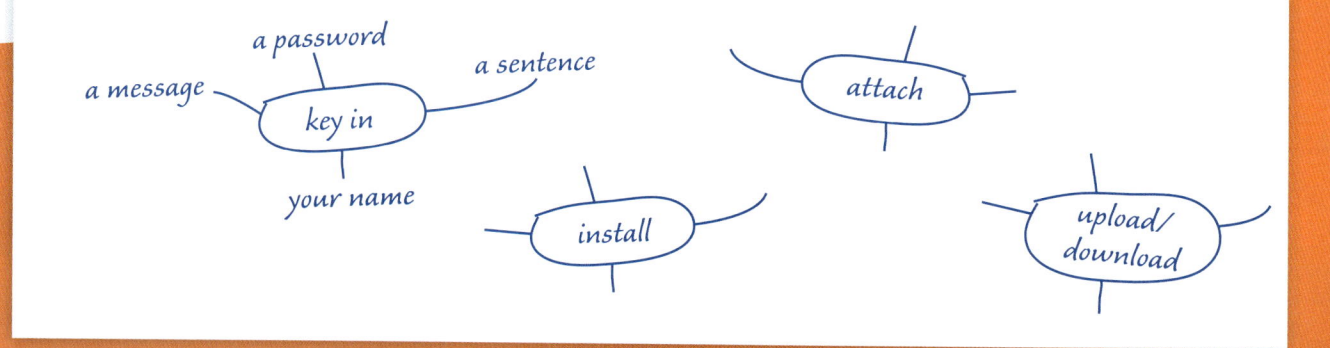

a message — a password — a sentence — your name → **key in**

attach

install

upload/download

4 SOCIAL NETWORKING

LISTENING

1 **Match the phrases with the definitions. Write the numbers 1–6.**

1 you get an error message | 2 an application closes down | 3 your screen goes blank | 4 you close a file without saving it first | 5 a programme freezes | 6 your hard disk crashes

a your computer monitor does not show any information any more
b a programme shuts down
c you lose all the changes you've just made
d information appears on your computer screen telling you about a problem
e the system that saves information on your computer suddenly stops working
f an application stops working, and the screen will not change no matter what you do

2 **SPEAKING** Work in pairs. Answer the questions.

1 Which of the problems in Exercise 1 have you experienced?
2 How do you usually solve computer problems?

3 ◁)) 1.29 **Listen to Hannah and her dad. Answer these questions.**

1 What's Hannah's dad trying to do?
2 What mistake has he made?

4 ◁)) 1.29 **Listen again. Look at the six sentences. Decide if each sentence is correct or incorrect. If it is correct, put a tick (✓) under A. If it is not correct, put a tick under B.**

	A	B
1 Hannah's dad likes gaming a lot.		
2 He's not happy when Hannah's brother spends his time playing computer games.		
3 Hannah says she'll tell her brother about their dad's interest in gaming.		
4 Dad didn't know that he had to create his own username and password.		
5 When Hannah tells him to choose a team, he's not very patient.		
6 Hannah reads out an error message that appears on the screen.		

GRAMMAR

all / some / none / any of them

1 **Complete the sentence. Look back at the article on page 39 to check.**

There were 500 people at the party, and
⁰ *some of them* were smashing windows and breaking potted plants.
Here are some important tips – ¹ _____ can guarantee 100% internet security, but
² _____ will help you to be safer online.

2 **Complete the rule with *things / more / none*.**

> **RULE:** We use the expressions *all / some / _____ / any of them* to refer back to a group (of _____ or people) and say _____ about it.

3 **Choose the correct words.**

1 My friends had a great time at my birthday party. *All / None* of them wanted to leave!
2 I have no idea which of these pens is Carla's. They all look exactly the same, so *any / some* of them could be hers.
3 These bikes all look good, but I'm sure *some / any* of them are better than others.
4 These T-shirts are really cool. *None / Any* of them would be fine for me.
5 These caps weren't expensive. I got *all / none* of them for £12.
6 We tried lots of different jeans, but *none / some* of them were the right size for me.
7 All the questions were really hard – I couldn't answer *none / any* of them!
8 Her songs are OK – I quite like *some / any* of them.

4 **Complete the sentences with *all / some / none / any*. (There may be more than one possible answer.)**

1 There are 32 students in Sarah's class. It's amazing that ___*all*___ of them like music, but _____ of them listen to jazz.
2 I like most American TV shows, but _____ of them are terrible!
3 OK, he scored three goals – but _____ of them were lucky!
4 The cakes that I made were horrible – we couldn't eat _____ of them, so we threw them all away.
5 My three brothers like IT, but _____ of them is as good with computers as my sister.
6 Look at those cameras. _____ of them are very cheap, but others are very expensive.

Workbook page 36

READING

1 Look at the mixed-up messages. Match them with the types of communication in the list. Write letters a–f.

1 text message ☐   4 online post ☐
2 text message ☐   5 email ☐
3 notice ☐   6 note ☐

2 Read the messages. Mark the correct answer A, B or C.

1 What should Emily's mum do?
   A Tell Benjamin to do the shopping for the family.
   B Warm up some food and buy a birthday present.
   C Make sure Benjamin knows Emily will be late.

2 What's the purpose of Benjamin's note?
   A To inform Emily of what Lucas said
   B To find out why Lucas phoned
   C To borrow a bike from Lucas

3 On her Facebook page, Emily
   A has posted photos of their trip.
   B asks Lucas what he thinks of the photos.
   C wants to say that she didn't like the trip.

4 The advert says the mountain bike
   A is almost new and in good condition.
   B is not the right bike for girls.
   C is in excellent condition, but expensive.

5 What should Lucas do?
   A Lower the price.
   B Give Emily a call.
   C Buy Emily a ring.

6 Lucas writes a text message
   A to invite Emily to join him again on Sunday.
   B to tell Emily that the weather is not good.
   C to invite his friends on a bike ride.

TRAIN TO THINK

Logical sequencing

1 Read the messages again. Work out a logical order. Write letters a–f in the right order.

☐ 1 ☐ 3 ☐ 5
☐ 2 ☐ 4 ☐ 6

2 SPEAKING Work in pairs. Compare your ideas with a partner. Discuss any differences.

---

a

Hi Mum,

I might not be at home before 6 this evening. Have seen an advert for a bike and would like to check it out. In case I'm late, Benjamin has promised to do the shopping. Good to have such a nice brother ;-) Looking forward to the pizza tonight. I'll be hungry as a wolf.

Love, Emily.

P.S.: You asked me to remind you it's dad's birthday on Tuesday. You ought to get him a nice present this year ;-)

b

MESSAGES
◀ Contacts

Hi Emily,
There was a phone call for you from someone called Lucas. He wanted to invite you for a bike ride on Saturday. He says you can use his bike and he'll borrow a friend's.
Oh, la la!
Benji

c

Great trip yesterday. Here are some photos of it. (1) Lucas and I getting ready for our bike ride. Note the big rucksack – everything in it for a wonderful picnic. (2) The picnic: Yummy!

The trip was great, but the weather wasn't too exciting. Pity we didn't get to the top. Had to turn back – fog and rain.

d

FOR SALE

Mountain bike, bought last month, used 3 times – perfect condition

Phone Lucas: 98576493

e

MESSAGES
Contacts

Hi E,
Best Saturday for a long time. I never knew rain and fog can be so much fun.
I'd like to try again next Sunday. You'd better join me if you don't want to break your promise ;-)!
L
P.S.: Love the photos on Facebook

f

▶ C ⌂

From: Emily
To: Lucas
Hi,
Have thought about it carefully. It's a cool bike, but £400 is a lot more than what I wanted to spend. Sorry!
Anyway, really nice to have met you. What you said about your bike tours sounded lovely. You should give me a ring some time if you want to ;-)
My phone: 97326797.
E

4 SOCIAL NETWORKING

GRAMMAR
Should(n't), had better, ought to

1 Complete these sentences from the messages on page 42. Then choose the correct words to complete the rule.

1. You _____ get him a nice present this year!
2. You _____ give me a ring some time if you want to.
3. You _____ join me if you don't want to break your promise.

> **RULE:** *Should*, *had better* and *ought to* are used to give ¹*advice / information*.
> - *Should* and *ought to* mean more or less the same, but we usually don't use *ought to* in questions and negative statements.
> - The meaning of **had better** is often a little stronger. The speaker wants to say that there are ²*positive / negative* consequences if you ignore the advice.
>
> These verbs ³*do / don't* use an auxiliary verb in the negative: *shouldn't*, *oughtn't to*, *had better not*.

2 Read the questions 1–6. Then match them to the correct answers a–f. Circle the correct word in each answer.

1. I've broken my friend's MP3 player. What should I do?
2. I've got toothache. What should I do?
3. I didn't do the test very well. What should I do?
4. I'd like to go climbing, but I've never done it before. What should I do?
5. I'm hungry. Should I eat some chocolate?
6. I'm angry with my brother. He said something I didn't like. What should I do?
7. This sweater my sister gave me looks terrible. I don't like it at all. What should I do?

a. You *should / shouldn't* eat it. Fruit is healthier.
b. You *should / shouldn't* tell him. It's best to be honest with him.
c. You'd *better / better not* return it to the shop. That would really hurt her feelings.
d. You *shouldn't / ought to* go back and study everything again.
e. You'd *better / shouldn't* get some training. It can be dangerous.
f. You *ought to / shouldn't* see a dentist.
g. You'd *better / shouldn't* say sorry the next time you meet your friend.

3 Look at these pictures. Write short dialogues with (serious or funny) answers giving advice.

1. **Boy** What should I do?
   Girl You should throw a sausage over the fence so the dog won't attack you.

> Workbook page 37

VOCABULARY
Language for giving advice

1 Look at the words and phrases below and answer the questions.

bad / good / practical / useful advice
advice about [something]
to take / follow [someone's] advice
to ignore [someone's] advice
to advise [someone] [to do something]
to advise against [something]
advisable

a. What's the difference between *advice* and *advise*?
b. Which of the phrases mean(s)
   – not to listen to somebody's advice?
   – do what somebody has advised you to do?
c. How do you say 'advisable' in your language?

2 Complete the sentences with phrases from Exercise 1. Use the correct verb forms.

1. I've told Peter he shouldn't post photos like that, but he has always _____ my _____ .
2. Should I buy a tablet or a laptop? Can you give me some _____ what's better?
3. He wants to become a web designer. His dad has _____ him to take a course. He should _____ that _____ .
4. My uncle has a heart problem. This web page _____ fatty foods.

> Workbook page 38

FUNCTIONS
Giving advice

SPEAKING Ask and answer questions with a partner.

1. Imagine you meet somebody who has never used a computer. What advice would you give them about social networking?
2. Are you good at giving advice? Say why (not) and give examples.
3. When do you find it difficult to follow someone's advice?

Culture

1 Look at the photos. What do they show?

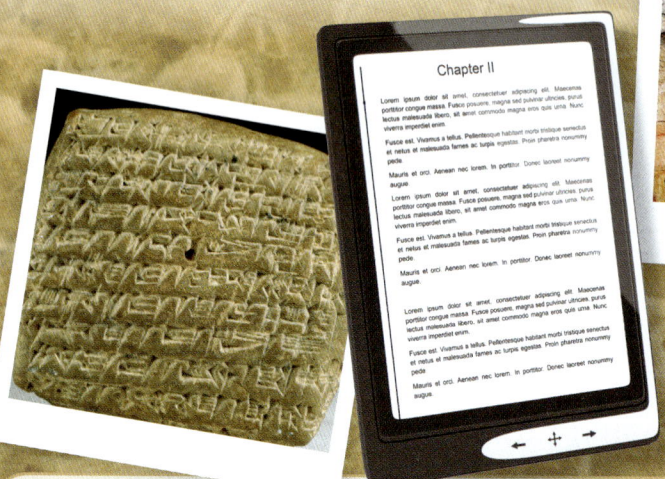

Communication through history

1 ☐

Cave paintings are the oldest pictures. Some of them, for example the beautiful images in the caves of Altamira in the north of Spain, are almost 30,000 years old. Many of these paintings show animals or hunting scenes. The images do not have written words. But when we look at them, we get an idea of the emotions the people felt when drawing them. The paintings tell stories of hopes and fears. They are an early form of communication.

2 ☐

Sometime between 4000 and 3000 BCE, people in Egypt and Mesopotamia developed the skill of writing. They engraved text on stone tablets first. But it was impossible to carry stones from place to place. The invention of papyrus allowed documents to be moved easily. Writing on papyrus made it easier to correct mistakes too. And do you know how they did that? When a scribe – the person who wrote the documents – made a mistake, they licked the ink off the papyrus before it got dry and made their corrections!

3 ☐

People made the first books from papyrus and from thin animal skins. Paper was invented in China as early as 105 CE. The quality of paper soon became very good. The world's oldest known printed book is from China too. It was published on May 11, 868 CE. In Europe, books were written manually until the middle of the 15th century when Johannes Gutenberg invented the printing press in Germany. Since that time, almost 140 million books have been published worldwide. For many people, one of life's greatest pleasures is spending a few hours in a bookshop browsing through the books.

4 ☐

Books will be around for many years, of course. But some people prefer reading e-books. They are easier to take with you when you travel, and you can download them instantly from the Internet. Now you can buy your books whenever you want without having to leave the comfort of your home.

2 🔊 1.30 Read and listen to the article again. Match the paragraph headings with the paragraphs. Write the letters a–f. Note that there are two headings you don't need.

a The invention of books by Gutenberg
b Early forms of written communication
c Books in their most modern form
d From stone tablets to the printing press
e Communication without reading and writing
f The history of book making

3 SPEAKING Work in pairs. Discuss the questions.

1 How important are books for you? Give reasons.
2 What book(s) have you read recently? How did you like them?
3 Do you prefer books or e-books? Give reasons.

Pronunciation
The short /ʌ/ vowel sound
Go to page 120.

4 SOCIAL NETWORKING

4 **VOCABULARY** Read the article again. Find words or phrases with the following meaning.

0. a large hole underground (paragraph 1) _cave_
1. happiness, love and anger (paragraph 1) _____
2. cut words into stone (paragraph 2) _____
3. paper made from plants (paragraph 2) _____
4. moved the tongue across something (paragraph 2) _____
5. produced (and sold) a book (paragraph 3) _____
6. a machine to make newspapers, books or magazines (paragraph 3) _____
7. looking through a book or magazine very quickly, without reading everything (paragraph 3) _____

WRITING
A web page giving advice

1 Read this information and decide who it would be important for. Then answer the questions.

1. Where do people use public computers?
2. What other examples not mentioned in the text can you think of?
3. Why should you never save a password on a public computer?
4. What's the problem with just closing the browser when you want to finish a session?

2 Rewrite the sentences by putting the words in brackets in the right position.

1. Read our advice. (carefully)
   Read our advice carefully.
2. Click 'Yes'. (don't)
3. Make you do not simply close the browser. (sure)
4. You should log out. (always)
5. Ask them to go somewhere else. (politely)

3 Are the sentences above used to give advice or to give an opinion? Match each of them with one of the situations below. Write the numbers 1–5.

a. when the system asks you 'Do you want to save the password?' ☐
b. when you want to leave a site ☐
c. to be smart and safe when using public computers ☐
d. if someone looks over your shoulder and watches you ☐
e. when you finish your session ☐

4 Match the content with the five sections of the text.

Introduction:	a Don't leave important information on the screen.
Bullet point 1:	b Log out properly.
Bullet point 2:	c Don't let people watch you.
Bullet point 3:	d What is the purpose of this text?
Bullet point 4:	e Don't save information.

How to use a public computer – safety tips

There are times when you may want to use a public computer, for example in an Internet café, a library or at an airport. That's when it's especially important to be smart and safe.

- **Don't save!** When you want to log into a social networking website or your web mail, the system will ask you, 'Do you want to save this password?' Don't click 'Yes' when you are working on a public computer.

- **Log out!** Make sure you do not simply close the browser when you want to leave a site. You should always "log out" of the site when you finish your session.

- **Close windows!** If you need to walk away from the computer for any reason, you should close all the windows on the computer first. Don't leave any information on the screen that other people shouldn't see.

- **Watch out!** Be careful about people looking at the screen over your shoulder. Ask them politely to go somewhere else so you can use the computer in private.

---

5 What would be important advice for good online behaviour? Make notes.

Here are some ideas:
- what (not) to share on social networks
- creating secure passwords and how to keep them safe
- what to do when you receive offensive comments on social websites
- what you should know about uploading photos on social networks

6 Write the text for a web page giving advice on good online behaviour (about 200 words).

- Use an introduction and bullet points to structure your text.
- Use language from Exercises 2 and 3 to give advice, and make sure your readers understand what situations your advice refers to.

CAMBRIDGE ENGLISH: Preliminary

THiNK EXAMS

READING
Part 2: Matching
Workbook page 42

1 These people are looking for a film to watch. Below are six film reviews. Decide which film, A–F, would be most suitable for these people.

1 Dawn loves thinking about the future. How will life be different? She's a huge fan of films that are set in a time many years from now. But she doesn't really enjoy films that are too frightening.

2 Paula's job is very boring so when she gets home she likes watching a good action film with lots of special effects, but she's not a fan of sci-fi. She also likes films with some exciting bits, too.

3 Keith is a romantic who enjoys a good love story but it must have a happy ending. He doesn't like serious films very much, and likes to have a laugh, too.

4 Lisa is not really a fan of fiction and only watches films about real life. She is interested in anything from history to nature to science as long as she learns something from it.

LISTENING
Part 4: True/false
Workbook page 35

2 🔊 1.33 You will hear a conversation between Ellen and her dad. Decide if each sentence is correct or incorrect. If it is correct, put a tick (✓) in the box under A for YES. If it is not correct, put a tick (✓) in the box under B for NO.

		A YES	B NO
1	Ellen's dad thinks she's been on the computer too long.		
2	Ellen's only been on the computer for 30 minutes today.		
3	Ellen was looking at a site about Queen Victoria.		
4	Ellen's dad wants to see what she's talking to Jenny about.		
5	Ellen's dad needs some help baking a cake.		
6	Ellen would like to see her dad working in the kitchen.		

HOT NEW FILMS ★

A The Invisible World
Using the most advanced camera technology in the world, this documentary takes us to places that have never been filmed before. From deep under the sea to inside the human body, this film contains some of the most amazing images you will ever see.

B The King Who Never Was
In 1936 Edward VIII decided to give up being king after less than a year so he could be with the woman he loved. This film revisits one of the most popular 'royal stories' of all time and mixes fact and fiction to create an interesting drama. It will keep audiences entertained but probably upset many historians.

C It Could Happen to You
Imagine waking up in a house that is not the house you went to sleep in. Imagine not recognising your children – even though they all seem to think you are their mum. This fascinating sci-fi takes us to a future world where people buy and sell memories.

D Will they? Won't they?
Ever since school, Jack and Jill have been best friends. But now they are in their twenties, and their feelings are changing. Is either of them brave enough to see that they are falling in love? Will they do something about it? Of course it is all OK in the end in this likeable but silly rom com.

E Countdown to Disaster
A speeding train is going to crash into a nuclear power station and no one can stop it. Or can they? Special agent Ryan has got an hour to stop the disaster but there's a problem, he has a bomb tied around his waist. Car chases, explosions and amazing special effects – this thriller has got it all.

F Tomorrow Now
The year is 2080 and for the last ten years Earth has been in contact with aliens. Today is the day that we finally welcome them to our planet. How will they change our lives and are they really as friendly as they seem? One of the scariest films you will see this year.

TEST YOURSELF

UNITS 3 & 4

VOCABULARY

1 Complete the sentences with the words in the list. There are two extra words.

comedy | thriller | download | ignore | upload | news
documentary | advice | advise | post | attachment | mode

1 If you're on a plane, you should activate flight _____ on your mobile phone.
2 There was a _____ programme on TV last night – the funniest programme I've ever watched!
3 I've got some great photos here. I'm going to _____ them onto my website tonight.
4 There was an interesting programme last night – a _____ about the history of my country.
5 Let me give you some _____ . Don't go and see that film – it's awful.
6 My father always watches the _____ on TV to see what's happening in the world.
7 I'm sure you think it's a good idea, but I'd _____ against it, to be honest.
8 I'm sending you a photo – it's in the _____ with this email.
9 If you want to talk to me, _____ a message on chat and I'll write back to you.
10 We gave him lots of advice, but he decided to _____ it!

/10

GRAMMAR

2 Complete the sentences with the words in the list.

best | better | no one | someone | none | everyone

1 I phoned, but _____ answered.
2 This is the _____ ice cream I've ever tasted.
3 I've got a problem and I need to talk to _____ , please.
4 I asked all my friends, but _____ of them knew the answer.
5 She plays the guitar _____ than me.
6 We had a great time. _____ enjoyed it.

3 Find and correct the mistake in each sentence.

1 He's a bit angry – I think you ought apologise to him.
2 The film isn't as good than the book.
3 There are six films on TV, and all of them is terrible!
4 It's the most bad party I've ever been to.
5 He runs more quick than me.
6 It's late. We'd better to go home now.

/12

FUNCTIONAL LANGUAGE

4 Complete the sentences with the words in the list.

against | everything | hand | help | ought | should | with | would

1 A Is _____ OK?
  B Yes, thanks. But perhaps I _____ sit down.
2 A Do you need any _____ ?
  B Well, yes, that _____ be great. Thanks!
3 A Could you help me _____ something? I want to borrow some money for a new guitar.
  B Well, you know, I'd advise _____ it. It's really not a good idea.
4 A Joe? This is heavy. Can you lend me a _____ ?
  B Of course, Mum. But you _____ to let me carry the heaviest bags!

/8

MY SCORE /30

22 – 30
10 – 21
0 – 9

47

5 MY LIFE IN MUSIC

OBJECTIVES

FUNCTIONS: asking about feelings; making helpful suggestions
GRAMMAR: present perfect continuous; present perfect simple vs. present perfect continuous
VOCABULARY: making music; musical instruments

READING

1 🔊 1.34 Listen. What type of music do you hear? Write the words in the pictures.

rap | jazz | opera | dance music | rock | pop

2 What other types of music can you think of?

3 **SPEAKING** Work in pairs. What kind of music do you like? Ask and answer questions.

Do you like ... ? I love/like/can't stand ...

I've never listened to ...

4 Look at the photos in the online forum on the next page and answer the questions.
  1 Which picture shows a busker?
  2 Which picture shows a talent show?
  3 Which of these people do you recognise?
  4 Do you know how they became famous?

5 Read the online forum quickly and check your ideas.

6 🔊 1.35 Read and listen to the online forum and answer the questions.
  1 What kind of shows are *The X Factor* and *The Voice*?
  2 Who won the first series of *The X Factor*?
  3 Where did One Direction finish in 2010's *The X Factor*?
  4 What was the first video Justin Bieber's mum put on the Internet?
  5 How old was Justin Bieber when Scooter Braun discovered him?
  6 How did Lily Allen get tens of thousands of fans?
  7 Why is busking good for a new musician?
  8 Where did Eric Clapton busk when he was starting out?

5 MY LIFE IN MUSIC

Singer songwriter: Any advice?

Hello. I'm a singer songwriter. I'm *good* and I'm going to make it big! Any advice????

Paulie asked 2 days ago Answers (3)

Answer #1 answered 4 hours ago

You could try going onto a show like *The X Factor* or *The Voice*. If you're as good as you say, then these TV talent shows will give you a chance. Of course, the competition will be really strong, and there can only be one winner. If you win it, you should have at least one hit album, but it's no guarantee that you will be successful for a long time. *The X Factor's* 2007 winner, Leona Lewis, has certainly become a big star, but who remembers the winner of the first series, Steve Brookstein? Maybe it's better not to win at all. In 2009 Olly Murs came second to Joe McElderry and is now much more famous. In 2010 One Direction came third, and the radio hasn't stopped playing them ever since.

Answer #2 answered 10 hours ago

Bands have been using the Internet for publicity for years now. It's cheap, quick and easy. Look at Justin Bieber. In 2007, when he was just 12, he entered a local singing competition and came second. His mum filmed him and put it on YouTube. Then she put on some more videos of him singing. In 2008 a talent scout called Scooter Braun accidentally clicked on one of Justin's videos. He really liked what he saw and went to meet the young Bieber. The rest is history. And then there's Lily Allen. She had a contract with a music label, but they were too busy with bigger artists to give her any attention. So she posted some of her music on MySpace. Soon, she had tens of thousands of fans, and lots of attention from her label. Thanks to the Internet, she became a star overnight.

Answer #3 answered 2 days ago

I've been writing songs since I was a teenager. I never really thought about making a record, but when I started my band I also started to get more serious about my music. We haven't been playing together very long, but people say we're really good. Now I'm really keen on making a career in music. I think the best advice is to start small and grow big. We've being doing a lot of busking in the streets and that's helped us get a good local following. We're now getting invitations from clubs in the area to come and play shows. Loads of famous people started out busking. Eric Clapton, one of the greatest guitarists in the world, busked on the streets of London when he was young.

THiNK VALUES

Following your dreams

1 Match these peoples with their dreams.

   1 Jessie is a really good artist. ☐
   2 Kylie loves acting. ☐
   3 David is great at football. ☐
   4 Lance has written a book. ☐

   a 'I want to get it published.'
   b 'I want to be in a play.'
   c 'I want to play professionally.'
   d 'I'd love to have an exhibition of my work.'

2 What should these people do to realise their dreams? Give advice. Make notes for each one.

   David / join club

3 **SPEAKING** Work in pairs. Compare your ideas.

   David should join a football club. He should practise for three hours every day.

4 **SPEAKING** Discuss these questions in small groups.

   1 What is your dream?
   2 What can you do to make it come true?

GRAMMAR
Present perfect continuous

1 **Complete the sentences with the correct form of the words in brackets. Check your answers in the online forum on page 49.**

1. I _____ (write) songs since I was a teenager.
2. We _____ (do) a lot of busking in the streets.
3. We _____ (not play) together very long.

2 **Match the example sentences below with the rules. Write the numbers 1–3.**

1. I've been learning the piano for two years.
2. I've been practising the piano since 10 am.
3. I've been playing the piano all day and I'm tired now.

> **RULE:** The present perfect continuous is used for actions happening over a period of time. We use it to:
> a emphasise how long an activity has been happening. The activity may or may not be complete.
> b talk generally about situations or activities that started in the past and are still continuing now.
> c talk about situations or activities that have stopped but have a result in the present.

3 **Choose the correct words.**

1. He's been *talking / talked* on the phone all morning.
2. I've *being / been* playing this game for hours now.
3. My dad *hasn't / haven't* been feeling well for a few days.
4. They've *been / being* studying since 10 o'clock.
5. We *haven't / hasn't* been living here for very long.
6. The dog's been *barked / barking* for half an hour.

4 **Complete the sentences. Use the correct form of the words and *for* or *since*.**

1. We're tired because we _____ (run) _____ hours.
2. I _____ (wait) for her _____ 40 minutes!
3. He _____ (watch) TV _____ 9 am.
4. She's red because she _____ (lie) in the sun _____ this morning.
5. They _____ (walk) in the rain _____ an hour and they're really wet.
6. Dad's exhausted because he _____ (work) in the garden _____ he got up.

Pronunciation
been: strong /biːn/ and weak /bɪn/
Go to page 120.

5 **SPEAKING** Work in pairs. Find out how long your partner has been doing these things.

1. living in their house?
2. learning English?
3. going to school?
4. walking?
5. talking?
6. playing an instrument?

> How long have you been playing the drums?

> For two years.

Workbook page 46

VOCABULARY
Making music

1 **Complete the story of Dymonde with the verbs in the list.**

won | start | entered | released | enter
downloading | writes | record | going | playing

Alan Bolan is a musician. He ¹_____ songs. One day he decided to ²_____ a band, so he put an advert in the paper. He soon found the band mates he was looking for. They practised hard and started ³_____ local gigs. A few months ago they decided to ⁴_____ a talent show. They ⁵_____ the competition, and their prize was a day in a recording studio. They used it to ⁶_____ a single called *Love Me Never*. They ⁷_____ the single on their website two weeks ago, and loads of people have been ⁸_____ it. It's already ⁹_____ the charts. Radio stations have been playing it loads, too. Next month they are ¹⁰_____ on tour all over the country. Rock critics are predicting a big future for Dymonde.

2 **SPEAKING** Work in pairs. Ask your partner about their favourite band. Use the expressions in Exercise 1.

> Who writes the songs?

> Have you downloaded any of their songs?

Workbook page 48

5 MY LIFE IN MUSIC

WRITING

Write the story of your favourite band.

Write about:
- how they started.
- how long they have been together.
- how they became successful.
- some of their famous hits.
- how long you have liked them.
- why you like them.

THiNK SELF-ESTEEM

Music and me

1 Do the quiz.

2 **SPEAKING** Work in pairs. Discuss the quiz.
- Do you agree or disagree with your score? Why?
- What music do you listen to when you are sad?
- What songs have special memories for you?
- What are your favourite song lyrics?
- How do you choose what clothes to buy?
- What music do your friends like?

LISTENING

1 ◁)) 1.38 Listen to the interview with Tom. What is he talking about?

2 ◁)) 1.38 Listen again and circle the correct answers. Sometimes there is more than one correct answer.

1 How does Tom feel when he hears a good new band?
  A really excited
  B worried
  C happy

2 Where does Tom hear new music?
  A on the radio
  B on the Internet
  C from his friends

3 Where does Tom get music?
  A He downloads it.
  B He borrows it from his friends.
  C He buys CDs.

4 When does he listen to music?
  A before he falls asleep
  B when he takes a shower
  C when he does his homework

5 How does Tom feel when he dances?
  A silly
  B happy
  C He doesn't dance.

3 ◁)) 1.39 Now listen to Sara answering the same questions and complete the sentences.

1 Sara mostly listens to …
2 Sara hears new music …
3 She downloads …
4 She always listens to music when …
5 When she dances she feels …

Does music rock your world? Could you live without it?

Take our quiz and find out just how important music is in your life.

For each question, choose the sentence that describes you best. Then work out your score and find out just how music mad you are.

1 A I only listen to music when I'm happy.
  B Music makes me feel better when I'm feeling down.
  C I listen to different music depending on how I feel.

2 A I have loads of memories connected to different songs.
  B I never listen to music from when I was younger.
  C I get bored with songs quickly.

3 A My musical taste influences the clothes I wear.
  B Music has nothing to do with fashion.
  C I don't really think about what I wear.

4 A I have the same musical tastes as my best friends.
  B I like different music from most of my friends.
  C I always know if I'm going to be friends with someone when they tell me their taste in music.

5 A I always listen to the lyrics in songs.
  B Melody is more important than lyrics.
  C Melody and lyrics are both really important in a song.

5–8: Music doesn't rule your world. You like it and you probably listen to it, but it's not so important.

9–11: Music plays an important part in your life, but it isn't the only thing that matters.

12–15: Music is your world and you would find it difficult to live without it. You live, sleep and breathe music.

Key
Q1 A – 1   B – 2   C – 3
Q2 A – 3   B – 2   C – 1
Q3 A – 3   B – 1   C – 2
Q4 A – 1   B – 3   C – 2
Q5 A – 1   B – 2   C – 3

READING

1 **SPEAKING** Work in pairs. How important are these things if you want to be a pop star? Put them in order 1–6. What other things can you think of?

☐ musical talent   ☐ a good manager   ☐ loyal fans
☐ good looks   ☐ luck   ☐ good songs

2 Read the article quickly. Which of these things does John Otway have?

John Otway – Rock's greatest failure

John Otway has been playing music and making records in the UK for more than 40 years. Over the years he has released more than ten albums. He has played hundreds of concerts. He has written two autobiographies. He has worked with some of the country's best musicians and he has even made a film about his life. But despite all of this, most people have never heard of him.

Otway released his first record in 1972, but it was the punk movement a few years later that really gave him his big chance. Otway wasn't the greatest musician but his songs were always fun, and his performances on stage were always entertaining – there was a good chance he would fall off the stage at least once in each show. The punks liked him, and in 1977 he had a small hit when his single *Really Free* made it to #27 in the UK top 40 charts. Otway really enjoyed his success but unfortunately, no more came. Not one of his records over the next 30 years was a hit.

Although he never had much commercial success, Otway had a lot of very loyal fans. When someone asked him what he would like for his 50th birthday, his reply was: 'A second hit.' His fans went out and bought as many copies of the new single *Bunsen Burner* as they could. And in October 2002, Otway finally saw his wish come true. In a chart that featured international superstars like Pink, Will Young and Oasis, *Bunsen Burner* made it to #9. Many high street shops refused to sell the record, saying that Otway was too old and unattractive for the teenage market. Otway didn't care. He celebrated his success with an appearance on TV's biggest music show *Top of the Pops*.

These days John Otway continues to play his music around the country, and there are always plenty of people who are happy to go and watch him perform. He's a great example for anyone who loves making music. You don't have to be young, good-looking (or even very talented) to enjoy a long career in the music business.

3 Read the article again. For each question, mark the correct answer A, B, C or D.

1 Which sentence best describes John Otway's popularity in the UK?
   A Many people do not know his name.
   B Everyone knows his name.
   C He was popular 30 years ago but he isn't popular any more.
   D He's quite popular with a lot of old people.

2 Which sentence best describes John Otway as a musician and performer?
   A He's a very talented song writer and guitarist.
   B He enjoys performing and making music.
   C He's a punk.
   D He's good at writing hit singles.

3 Why did some shops not sell his single *Bunsen Burner*?
   A Because they thought it was terrible
   B Because it wasn't a very big hit
   C Because John Otway didn't want them to have it
   D Because they thought no one would buy it

4 What is the message of the text?
   A You don't have to be young to be a successful pop star.
   B It's important to be successful.
   C Do what you love doing.
   D Musicians get better as they get older.

5 MY LIFE IN MUSIC

GRAMMAR
Present perfect simple vs. present perfect continuous

1 Complete the sentences with the verb *play* in the correct tense. Look at the article on page 52 to check your answers.

1 He _____ music for more than 40 years.
2 He _____ hundreds of concerts.

2 Complete the rules and match them with the examples sentences in Exercise 1.

> **RULES:**
> • Use the present perfect _____ to talk about an action that is not finished.
> • Use the present perfect _____ to stress the *finished result* of a completed activity and the *amount* completed.

3 Complete the sentences with the phrases in the list.

'␣ve been having | Has … been preparing
'␣ve been watching | '␣ve eaten | haven't taken
'␣ve played | '␣ve been playing | '␣s been writing
'␣s written | '␣s made

1 Sarah _____ more than 200 poems. She _____ poems since she was eight.
2 I _____ piano lesson for three years. I _____ any piano exams yet.
3 I _____ football since I was five. I _____ for three different teams.
4 We _____ films all evening. We _____ three bags of popcorn between us.
5 Mum _____ more than 100 sandwiches. _____ she _____ for the party all morning?

4 Complete the sentences using the correct forms of the verbs.

1 He _____ autographs since he was ten. He _____ over 500. (collect)
2 Jade _____ over 5,000 photos on her phone. She _____ them ever since she bought it. (take)
3 Mum _____ since 6 am. She _____ over 400 km. (drive)
4 We _____ for an hour. We _____ more than 2 km! (swim)
5 Mr Bosworth _____ more than 2,000 children. He _____ since he was 22. (teach)
6 They _____ apples all day. They _____ hundreds! (pick)

➜ Workbook page 47

VOCABULARY
Musical instruments

1 Match the instruments with the words in the list. Write 1–8 in the boxes.

1 drums | 2 bass guitar | 3 saxophone | 4 piano
5 violin | 6 trumpet | 7 keyboard | 8 guitar

A ☐ B ☐ C ☐ D ☐ E ☐ F ☐ G ☐ H ☐

2 🔊 1.40 Listen. Which instrument is playing?

1 *bass guitar*

➜ Workbook page 48

SPEAKING

Work in pairs. Answer the questions.

1 Do you play an instrument? If yes, how long have you been playing it? If no, would you like to play an instrument?
2 Which of the instruments in Exercises 1 and 2 do you really like? Which instruments don't you like?
3 What famous musicians can you think of? How long have they been playing music? Have you seen them playing live?

PHOTOSTORY: episode 3

Pop in the park

1 Look at the photos and answer the questions.
  1 What's Luke's problem?
  2 What suggestions do Megan and Ryan make?

2 🔊 1.41 Now read and listen to the photostory. Check your answers.

MEGAN Have a look at this. There's going to be a concert in our park.
OLIVIA Wow – The Unwanted! I've just heard their new song. I love it.
RYAN And Daddy D – awesome! I'm so going to go.
MEGAN Me, too. I can't wait.

OLIVIA What's up, Luke? Aren't you excited?
LUKE Not really. Well I am, but…
RYAN What? What's the matter?
LUKE I'm just a bit upset. I mean, where am I going to get £20 from? I've run out of money. I spent all my money for the month on that new video game I told you about.

MEGAN Can't you ask your dad?
LUKE No way. He won't lend me money. Especially for a concert. He hates my music.
OLIVIA Tell me about it. My parents can't stand my music, either.
RYAN But listen, why don't you sell something?
LUKE I haven't got anything I want to sell.
OLIVIA Nothing at all?
LUKE No, nothing.

LUKE Well, there's no point in getting upset. I can't go and that's that.
RYAN Well, if you say so.
OLIVIA Come on, Luke. I'm sure we'll sort something out.
RYAN This cat's been following us for ages. Hey, kitty!
MEGAN She's so cute. But you'll have to stay here now. You can't come to school with us.

5 MY LIFE IN MUSIC

DEVELOPING SPEAKING

3 Work in pairs. Discuss what happens next in the story. Write down your ideas.

We think that Ryan finds some money in the street and gives it to Luke.

4 ▶ EP3 Watch to find out how the story continues.

5 Complete the sentences with the names in the list. There are two extra names.

Sophie | Lucky | Tiddles | Sammy | Tiger | Lucy

1 Ryan thinks the cat's name should be _____ .
2 Olivia calls the cat _____ .
3 Luke calls the cat _____ .
4 The cat's real name is _____ .

6 Why do the kids choose those names?

PHRASES FOR FLUENCY

1 Find the expressions 1–6 in the story. Who says them? How do you say them in your language?

1 I can't wait.
2 What's up?
3 No way.
4 Tell me about it.
5 There's no point in …
6 If you say so.

2 Complete the conversations. Use the expressions in Exercise 1.

1 A Hey Mandy. ¹_____ ?
  B I'm tired! I had problems with the homework last night.
  A ²_____ ! I took four hours to finish it! And I think I got some things wrong.
  B Me too. Oh well. ³_____ worrying about it. Let's give it to the teacher, and see.

2 A The Cup Final's on TV tonight. ⁴_____ !
  B I know. It's really exciting. Do you want to come and watch it with me, at my house?
  A ⁵_____ ! Your television's terrible.
  B Well, ⁶_____ . But I think our TV's really good.

WordWise
Phrasal verbs with *out*

1 Complete each of these sentences from the unit so far with a word from the list.

come | find | run | went | started | sort

1 Lots of famous musicians _____ out playing on the streets of London.
2 His fans _____ out and bought all the copies.
3 Their new single has just _____ out.
4 Come on, Luke. I'm sure we'll _____ something out.
5 I've _____ out of money.
6 Listen and _____ out how the story ends.

2 Match the phrases and the definitions.

1 start out   a discover
2 find out   b begin your working life
3 go out   c leave your house
4 come out   d appear in a shop so people can buy it
5 run out   e find an answer or solution to a problem
6 sort out   f use all of something

3 Complete the sentences with the correct form of the verbs in Exercise 2.

1 John isn't here. He _____ about 20 minutes ago.
2 It's a really old film. I think it _____ about 2005.
3 We need to go to the supermarket – we _____ of milk.
4 The police are trying to _____ who started the trouble last night.
5 We had some problems with the computer, but we _____ them _____ yesterday.
6 She's a famous singer now, but she _____ as a dancer.

→ Workbook page 49

FUNCTIONS
Asking about feelings

1 Match the questions and the answers.

1 What's up Luke?   a Not great.
2 Is something the matter? b Yes, I'm fine.
3 How are you feeling?   c Nothing.
4 Are you OK?   d I'm just a bit upset.

Helpful suggestions

2 ROLE PLAY Work in pairs. Student A: go to page 127. Student B: go to page 128. Look at the role cards and do the role play.

55

6 MAKING A DIFFERENCE

OBJECTIVES

FUNCTIONS: expressing surprise and enthusiasm
GRAMMAR: *will* (*not*), *may* (*not*), *might* (*not*) for prediction; first conditional; *unless* in first conditional sentences
VOCABULARY: the environment; verbs to talk about energy

READING

1 Match the words and phrases in the list with the pictures. Write 1–6 in the boxes.

1 a beautiful beach | 2 a dirty beach
3 clean water | 4 an attractive landscape
5 an endangered species | 6 a polluted river

2 **SPEAKING** Work in pairs. Which of the above are easy / difficult / impossible to find in your town or country? Discuss using the expressions below.

- There is / are lots of … in …
- I think 50 years ago there were more / fewer …
- It would be good to have more …

3 **SPEAKING** Tell your partner about places you have visited. Which of the things in Exercise 1 did you see?

Years ago I visited …   I saw lots of …

I was surprised / disappointed to see …

4 🔊 1.42 Look at the sentences below about the environment. Read and listen to the article to decide if each sentence is correct or incorrect. If it's correct, mark it A. If it's incorrect, mark it B.

1 Black rhinos are far more endangered than tigers.
2 At the beginning of the last century there were ten times more tigers than now.
3 The fishing industry gets more money for fish that are in danger than for the ones that are not.
4 The fishing laws are very strict, and the fishing industry keeps to them.
5 Financial interests play a big role in deforestation.
6 Sea levels rise as sea temperatures fall.

5 Rewrite the false sentences from Exercise 4 to make them true.

A   B   C   D   E   F

56

6 MAKING A DIFFERENCE

Hot topic: THE ENVIRONMENT

This week, four experts share with us what they think the key challenges for the world's environment will be in the future. As always, we are curious to get our readers' reactions. So tell us what you think.

1 Endangered species

The black rhino in Africa is in serious danger of becoming extinct. This is because some people think rhino horn has special powers. They pay enormous sums of money for it. So people kill rhinos and sell their horns. Tigers are in serious danger, too. At the beginning of the 20th century, there were about 100,000 tigers. Now there are only about 3,000 left. In a few years' time, there might not be any tigers left at all! These are just two examples. Many other animals are endangered, too. Some of them may be gone forever very soon.
Joc Wagner, Cape Town

2 Overfishing

It's not looking good for the fish population. Certain species are in danger, and there aren't many of them in the sea where fishermen usually go. Fishing ships are therefore going further and further out into the oceans. They try to get the rare species because they can get better prices for them. If things go on like this, 40 years from now there won't be any fish left in the seas. It's not too late yet, but it may be soon. The oceans need much stricter laws and a fishing industry that keeps to them. *Rick Cavendish, San Diego*

3 Deforestation

About 30% of the world's land is still covered with forests. But every year, we lose areas as big as the country of Panama. Big companies earn millions from producing wood, paper and cardboard from the trees. Forests are also cut down to make more space for growing crops such as soya or creating huge cattle farms. The consequences of deforestation are dramatic and partly responsible for climate change. About 70% of the world's land animals and plants live in forests. If we lose the forests, we will lose millions of species. *Alejandro Silvas, Quito*

4 Rising levels of sea water

Over the last 20 years or so, sea water temperatures have been going up. As a consequence, the ice caps around the poles have started to melt, and sea levels have started to rise. If this doesn't stop, the water will rise further and may flood many islands. Then some countries like the Maldives won't be there any more. There is also a danger that some huge low-lying coastal cities might end up below the sea. It's hard to imagine what the consequences of such changes might be. *Gajkaran Sanu, New Delhi*

THiNK VALUES

Caring for the world

1 Read and tick (✓) the values that are linked with the problems discussed in the article.

- [ ] 1 We have responsibilities towards future generations.
- [ ] 2 People have a right to express their opinions freely.
- [ ] 3 All people have a right to live in peace.
- [ ] 4 Our behaviour can make a difference.
- [ ] 5 Humans have a responsibility to protect endangered species.
- [ ] 6 We must change our behaviour towards our planet.

2 **SPEAKING** Work in pairs. Say what you think about the values.

I think number ... is an important value.

It says ... and I agree that ... . Do you agree?

Yes. If we don't ... , then future generations will/won't ...

Politicians/People/Everybody should ...

I think it's good that ...

GRAMMAR
will (not), may (not), might (not) for prediction

1 **Complete the examples from the article on page 57. Underline other examples of *will*, *won't*, *may (not)* and *might (not)*. Then complete the rule.**

1 In a few years' time, there _____ any tigers left.
2 Some animals _____ forever very soon.
3 If we lose the forests, we _____ millions of species.

> **RULE:** Use *will* or [1]_____ to express future certainty, and [2]_____ (*not*) or *might* (*not*) to express future possibility.

2 **Complete the sentences. Use *will* or *won't* and the verbs in brackets.**

1 I'm not exactly sure, but I think she _____ (be) home by eight o'clock at the latest.
2 I wonder if people _____ (live) on other planets in the future.
3 I'm worried about him coming with us. I'm sure he _____ (like) any of the people at the party.
4 Who do you think _____ (win) the next World Cup?
5 It's getting cloudy. Do you think it _____ (start) raining soon?
6 Oh, don't worry about my parents. I'm sure they _____ (be) angry.

3 **Read the sentences and circle the correct words.**

1 Don't worry I *will / might* pick you up at 7.
2 The weather's a real problem. We *may / may not* be able to go for a walk.
3 She's not feeling well at all. She *might / might not* have to stay at home.
4 It *may / may not* be cold later so take a jumper with you.
5 It's my dad's birthday tomorrow. My wife and I are going to visit him, so we definitely *won't / might not* be here.
6 I'd like to get up and watch the sunrise with you, but I *may / won't* just sleep instead.

4 **SPEAKING** Work in pairs. Think about your next weekend. Talk about:
- a sport you will / won't do
- someone you may / may not see
- a film you might / might not watch

→ Workbook page 54

VOCABULARY
The environment

1 **Match the words with their definitions.**

1	extinct	a	official rules that say what people are allowed and not allowed to do
2	laws	b	to change from solid to liquid (for example, from ice to water)
3	waste	c	a large amount of water covering an area that is usually dry
4	melt	d	not existing any more
5	flood	e	things that make water, air, and the ground unclean
6	pollution	f	material that people throw away because they do not want or need it any more

2 **SPEAKING** Work in pairs. Ask and answer questions.

1 Which animals do you know that are extinct or in danger of extinction?
2 What laws to protect the environment are there in your country?
3 What problems with waste are there where you live?
4 What might happen if the ice around the north and south poles melts?
5 Are floods common in your country?
6 Are the air and water very polluted in your area? What could your class do to help fight pollution?

3 **◁)) 1.43** Match the words in the list with the pictures. Write 1–4 in the boxes. Then listen, repeat and check.

1 smog | 2 recycling | 3 litter | 4 rubbish

A B C D

4 **Think about the environment in your country. Make notes.**

some rivers polluted
air pollution from factories

6 MAKING A DIFFERENCE

5 **SPEAKING** Work in pairs. Look at your notes from Exercise 4. Make predictions for the next 30 years. Which environmental issues concern you the most? Then report to the class.

> *Some of the rivers in our country are polluted, for example … We think this will create big problems for the fish, and …*

> *In some parts of the country, for example in … , the air is polluted. We think this will change. There will be stricter laws so there won't be …*

Workbook page 56

LISTENING

1 Read the headlines in the online newspaper story and look at the images. Write down six words you might find in the article.

Incredible Edible
Carrots in the car park
Radishes on the roundabout
The deliciously eccentric story of the town growing ALL its own vegetables.

2 ◉ 1.44 You are going to listen to a story about a town named Todmorden. Use the information from the newspaper story and your imagination to say what you think is special about it. Then listen and check.

3 ◉ 1.44 Listen again and answer the questions.
1 What's the project 'Incredible Edible' all about?
2 Who takes part in the project?
3 Who had the idea?
4 How did they get the idea?
5 How did people react?

4 Do you think the experiment will last? Why or why not? Would you like to see a similar experiment in your town or neighbourhood?

FUNCTIONS
Expressing surprise and enthusiasm

1 ◉ 1.44 Listen to the radio programme again. The phrases below can be used to express enthusiasm. Tick the ones that the reporter uses.

- [ ] What a brilliant idea!
- [ ] That sounds wonderful!
- [ ] How exciting!
- [ ] That's amazing! (wonderful! etc.)
- [ ] Wow!
- [ ] Oh, really?
- [ ] Incredible! (Cool! Fascinating! etc.)

2 Put the dialogue in order. Read it out with a partner.

- [ ] A He has offered me a role in his next film.
- [ ] A I'm only going to meet Stephen Spielberg.
- [1] A I'm going to California this summer.
- [ ] A Three hours.
- [ ] B Cool!
- [ ] B Oh, really? Only three hours. Why's that?
- [ ] B How exciting! What are you going to talk about?
- [ ] B Wow! That sounds exciting. How long are you going to stay there?

3 **SPEAKING** Practise dialogues with a partner. A says something surprising, B reacts using one of the expressions from Exercise 1 and asks a question. A says something surprising again, etc. Use your own ideas, or the ones here.

- go to the moon
- meet Bradley Cooper
- have an important meeting
- see an alien
- only eat white food
- stay up all night

TRAIN TO THINK

Different perspectives

1 Read these different texts. Match them with the text types in the list. Write numbers 1–4. Give your reasons. There are two text types you don't need to use.

- note ☐
- diary entry ☐
- text message ☐
- newspaper article ☐
- informative leaflet ☐
- adventure story ☐

2 **SPEAKING** Work in pairs. Discuss who the texts are for and what their purpose is.

I think text 1 is probably for …
I think somebody wrote it in order to …

1 This morning we took part in the Incredible Edible project. I was so proud when I saw that all of the 27 children in my class had brought vegetable plants …

2 Meeting the guys who want to plant vegetables by the football field at 5… Hope to CUL8R. S.

3 … to buy OUR vegetables. They come from local farms in the neighbourhood. They are organic and fresh – and you don't have to pick them yourself. Prices are reasonable, the quality is high!

4 Reporter Mac Hendon has learned that the council will soon publish a list of spare land that can be used by the Incredible Edible project. It has been …

READING

1 Read the text. What type of text is it? Choose from the types in the exercise above. Who might this text be for?

Small changes, BIG consequences
6 things you can do to help the environment

1. Don't leave your DVD player, your computer or other electrical appliances on standby. If you switch off your TV completely when you've stopped watching, it won't use any electricity. People think that a gadget on standby uses only the electricity for that 'little red light'. Not true!

2. When you charge your mobile, disconnect the charger from the phone when the battery is fully charged. Otherwise you're wasting energy.

3. If you reuse your shopping bags when you go to the supermarket, you'll save money. If you keep them and take them with you the next time you go shopping, you won't need new bags. Don't forget that a lot of energy is needed to produce plastic bags, and plastic waste is a danger for the environment. Unless people stop throwing plastic away, the environment will suffer even more.

4. Don't let the water run while you're brushing your teeth. If you turn it off and use a cup of water to rinse your mouth, you'll save a lot of water!

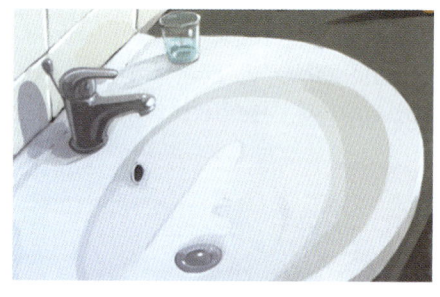

5. Make sure none of the taps in your house drip. If a tap drips, it wastes three or more litres of water a day.

6. Think before you throw things away, and tell your family to do the same. They may not want to use an old mobile, computer or MP3 player any more. That doesn't mean those things should end up in the litter bin. If they go to a charity instead, other people might find them very useful.

2 **SPEAKING** Work in pairs. Cover up the text and try to complete the sentences.

1 A gadget on standby uses …
2 When your phone is fully charged you should …
3 Plastic bags are a problem for the environment because … So we should …
4 When you brush your teeth it's better to …
5 Taps should never …
6 Before you throw something away, ask yourself who might …

3 Read the tips again. Which of the suggestions …

- do you already do?
- would be easy for you to start doing?
- would be difficult for you to follow?

6 MAKING A DIFFERENCE

GRAMMAR
First conditional; *unless* in first conditional sentences

1 Complete the sentences with the correct form of the verbs. Look at the leaflet on page 60 and check your answers. Then choose the right answers to make the rules.

1 If you switch off your TV completely when you have stopped watching, it _____ (not use) any electricity.
2 If you reuse your shopping bags when you go to the supermarket, you _____ (save) money.
3 Unless people stop throwing plastic away, the environment _____ (suffer) even more.

> **RULE:** We use the first conditional to talk about the consequences of a ¹*possible / impossible* future action.
> - Condition clause: *if* + present simple
> - Result clause: *will / won't* + main verb
>
> The condition clause can come before or after the result clause.
>
> *Unless* means ²*only if / if not*.

2 Match the parts of the sentences.

1 Unless someone lends me a bit of money,
2 I'll only be able to go to the concert
3 They won't pass the exam
4 Won't she miss the train

a if my dad drives me there.
b if she doesn't leave for the station now?
c I won't be able to take the bus home.
d unless they study hard.

3 Write first conditional sentences. Then decide in which of them you could use *unless*.

0 environment / suffer / if / we not recycle more
The environment will suffer if we don't recycle more. The environment will suffer unless we recycle more.

1 if / I give this phone / charity / they find someone who needs it
2 if / this tap not stop dripping / how much water / we waste in a day?
3 situation / become worse / if they not change behaviour
4 Look – battery full! / if you not disconnect charger / you waste energy
5 if she read this book / she understand situation better
6 if / you not stop shouting / I not listen any more

4 Complete the questions. Use the correct form of the verbs.

0 What _will_ you _do_ if they _don't help_ you? (do / not help)
1 If you _____ , _____ you _____ good marks in your test? (not study / get)
2 Unless the weather _____ really bad on Sunday, we _____ to the beach. (be / go)
3 If she _____ you to her birthday party, _____ you _____ her a present? (invite / buy)
4 She _____ him unless he _____ her very nicely. (not help / ask)
5 If I _____ to visit you, _____ you _____ me around your town? (come / show)

5 **SPEAKING** Work in pairs. Ask and answer questions using the first conditional. Use your own ideas or the ones here.

1 What will you do if it rains all weekend?
2 What will you buy if you get some extra money this month?
3 What will you do tonight if you don't have any homework?

> Workbook page 55

VOCABULARY
Verbs to talk about energy

1 🔊 2.02 Match the verbs with their definitions. Write 1–8. Listen and check.

1 to reuse | 2 to throw away | 3 to recycle
4 to waste | 5 to charge | 6 to disconnect
7 to save | 8 to leave on standby

a not to switch an appliance off completely so it is ready to be used at any time
b to collect and treat rubbish in order to produce useful materials that can be used again
c to fill up an empty battery again
d to get rid of something
e to stop something from being wasted
f to stop the connection between an electrical appliance and the power source
g to use something again
h to use too much of something or use it incorrectly

2 **SPEAKING** Work in pairs. Discuss these questions.

1 Do you waste a lot of energy? What could you do to save energy?
2 What things do you reuse?
3 What things do you recycle? Do you think there is enough recycling done where you live? Why?

> Workbook page 56

Culture

1. Look at the picture. Do you know what this is?

2. 🔊 2.03 Read and listen to the article. What animals does it mention?

STOP! BEFORE IT'S TOO LATE

The Himalayas

Why should we care?
The Himalayan mountains in South Central Asia contain many of the world's tallest **peaks**, including Mount Everest. They also contain the biggest number of **glaciers** after the North and South poles. Three of the greatest rivers in the world start from these mountains: the Ganges, the Indus and the Yangtze. These rivers provide water to a billion people in Asia.

What's happening?
The biggest danger to the Himalayas is **global warming**, which is melting the glaciers fast. There is also a huge problem with deforestation in the mountains. Many species of animals such as the tiger, the rhino and the snow leopard are in danger.

The Galapagos Islands

Why should we care?
The Galapagos Islands are one of the most amazing places on Earth. These **tiny** islands are 1,000 km from Ecuador in the Pacific, and contain many species of plants and animals that are found nowhere else in the world, among them the giant tortoise, the Galapagos penguin and the Galapagos sea lion. They are also famous because the scientist Charles Darwin spent time there studying the wildlife.

What's happening?
The Galapagos Islands are very **fragile**. The greatest dangers to them include overfishing, pollution and tourism. There is also a threat of animals from other parts of the world arriving on the islands and killing the local wildlife.

The Amazon

Why should we care?
The Amazon in Brazil is the largest tropical rainforest in the world. It is home to 10% of the world's wildlife. The Amazon River is the largest in the world and contains the most freshwater fish on the planet. It is also home to 350 different **tribes**. But perhaps most importantly, it provides between 25 and 30% of the world's oxygen.

What's happening?
The biggest **threat** is deforestation. This happens to make space for farm land and to have wood. As a result, many animals are endangered, among them the golden lion tamarin and the jaguar. Since 1950 we have lost more than 17% of the Amazon rainforest. We can't afford to lose any more.

The Great Barrier Reef

Why should we care?
The Great Barrier Reef, off the eastern coast of Australia, is over 2,000 km long. It is the only living **organism** on the planet that you can see from space. It is home to 1,500 different types of fish, 400 different types of coral, 215 different types of birds and six different types of turtle.

What's happening?
We have already lost 10% of all the coral, but scientists **fear** that we will lose 70% more in the next 40 years. The greatest dangers to the reef are pollution and overfishing.

3. **SPEAKING** Work in pairs. Say what these numbers in the article refer to.
    a 1,000,000,000
    b 350
    c 17
    d 1,000
    e 2,000
    f 70

    A billion – that's the number of people in Asia that get their water from the Ganges, the Indus and the Yangtze.

4. **SPEAKING** Can you think of any other areas of the world that are in danger from environmental damage?

6 MAKING A DIFFERENCE

5 VOCABULARY Match the words in bold in the article with the definitions. Write the words.

0 groups of people who live together, usually outside towns and cities, and have the same language, culture, and history *tribes*
1 the rise in temperature of the Earth's climate _____
2 a living thing _____
3 are afraid _____
4 weak / easy to damage _____
5 large masses of ice that move slowly _____
6 the tops of mountains _____
7 very small _____
8 something that will probably harm or destroy something else _____

Pronunciation
/f/, /v/, /b/ consonant sounds
Go to page 120.

WRITING
An article for the school magazine

1 Read this article from a school magazine. Answer the questions.

1 What is its purpose?
2 How has the river changed?
3 What are the main reasons for the problems?
4 What will happen if the situation doesn't change?
5 What should be done?

2 Put the words in the correct order to make sentences from the article. Then go through it and underline the evidence the writer uses to support each of these statements.

1 so / the / beautiful / once / Quiller River / was
2 situation / alarming / is / the
3 the / river / and / look at / banks / just

3 Match the sentence halves. Which of them talk about possible consequences? Which are suggestions? Which are predictions?

1 If politicians wake up and we all do something,
2 We need stricter laws
3 In a few years' time
4 So I really think politicians
5 The situation will be even worse in a few years

a to protect our river.
b unless factories stop polluting.
c we might once again be able to enjoy the river.
d should do something about it.
e all the fish may be dead.

4 The article has four paragraphs. Which of them …

a expresses the writer's hope that the situation will be better in the future?
b introduces the topic?
c describes problems and says what should be done?
d describes problems, says what will happen if nothing is done and what should be done?

The sad story of a once beautiful river

The Quiller River was once so beautiful that there is even a song about it. And now?

The situation is alarming. There are lots of factories along the river. Newspapers have recently reported that the water in the river is totally polluted. There are hardly any fish left, and the water itself smells terrible. The situation will be even worse in a few years unless factories stop polluting the water. So I really think politicians should do something about it. We need stricter laws to protect our river.

And just look at the river banks. They are covered in litter. It seems that there are lots of people who throw their waste into the river. This must stop! We should all get together and help clean up the river banks.

If politicians wake up and we all do something, we might once again be able to enjoy the beauty of the river. Let's hope it's not too late.

5 Choose one of these environmental problems and make notes about what the situation is now, possible consequences and what should be done.

a one of the problems mentioned in this unit, for example, deforestation in the Amazon
b an environmental issue in your town or country

6 Write an article for your school magazine raising awareness about the environmental issue you have chosen.

- Find a good title.
- Write an introduction that catches the reader's interest.
- Describe what the problems are, what you think the consequences might be and what should be done.

CAMBRIDGE ENGLISH: Preliminary

THiNK EXAMS

READING
Part 5: Four-option multiple-choice cloze

1 Read the text below and choose the correct word for each space.
For each question, mark the correct letter A, B, C or D.

I'm an eco-counsellor at my school. It's a job I have ⁰_____ doing for 6 months, and it's something I enjoy a lot. As an eco-counsellor I'm responsible ¹_____ making sure that our school does as much ²_____ it can for our environment.

Altogether there are six of us. We have ³_____ meeting once every two weeks, and we discuss what we can do ⁴_____ encourage students to think about their behaviour and how to be more environmentally friendly. For example, last month we ⁵_____ a plan to stop littering around the school. We put up posters ⁶_____, and I even made a small speech in a school assembly. It's already had an amazing impact, and you ⁷_____ ever see any rubbish on the floor in a the school. We ⁸_____ decided to get students to think about recycling. We have now got different bins for glass, paper and plastics in ⁹_____ classroom. If we all ¹⁰_____ the bins, our school will be a cleaner, healthier place.

0	A	being	B	be	(C)	been	D	was
1	A	for	B	of	C	in	D	by
2	A	so	B	than	C	for	D	as
3	A	a	B	–	C	an	D	the
4	A	for	B	to	C	so	D	about
5	A	did	B	made	C	ran	D	make
6	A	everywhere	B	nowhere	C	anywhere	D	somewhere
7	A	often	B	sometimes	C	hardly	D	occasionally
8	A	too	B	also	C	as well	D	else
9	A	all	B	some	C	every	D	no
10	A	using	B	have used	C	are using	D	use

WRITING
Part 1: Sentence transformations

Workbook page 17

2 Here are some sentences about music.
For each question, complete the second sentence so it means the same as the first.
Use no more than three words.

0 We moved into this house two years ago.
We ___*have been*___ living in this house for two years.

1 Their new CD isn't as good as the last one.
Their last CD was _____ their new one.

2 Two hours ago he got into the pool and started swimming.
He _____ for two hours.

3 If you don't practise, you'll never be a good drummer.
You won't be a good drummer _____ practise.

4 They came on stage at 8 pm and they're still playing now two hours later.
They _____ on stage for two hours now.

5 There a 50% chance that I'll go to the show on Saturday.
I _____ to the show on Saturday.

64

TEST YOURSELF

UNITS 5 & 6

VOCABULARY

1 Complete the sentences with the words in the list. There are two extra words.

release | standby | tour | extinct | flood | record
enter | waste | charge | melt | download | throw away

1 Is it OK if I _____ my mobile phone in your room?
2 It's getting warm now, so I think the snow will _____ soon.
3 Don't _____ water. You shouldn't stay in the shower for more than four minutes!
4 Our WiFi connection is really slow. It takes a long time to _____ songs.
5 They've recorded a new CD, and they're going to _____ it next week.
6 You can't win the competition if you don't _____ it!
7 After the band released their new record, they went on _____ for three months.
8 If it carries on raining like this, there might be a _____ tonight.
9 There aren't many of these animals left in the world. They could be _____ in a few years.
10 Don't switch it off completely – leave it on _____, OK?

/10

GRAMMAR

2 Complete the sentences with the words in the list.

unless | if | have played | have been playing | won't | might not

1 I didn't study for the test. I _____ pass it, I'm sure!
2 Sorry, Mum. My shoes are really dirty. I _____ football in the park.
3 We won't go for a walk _____ it rains.
4 I don't feel very well, so I _____ go to school tomorrow. I'm not sure.
5 I'll never finish this homework _____ you help me. Please!
6 Everyone in the team is really tired. We _____ three games this week already!

3 Find and correct the mistake in each sentence.

1 He's being working here for over ten years.
2 If it will rain, we'll stay at home.
3 I've been making fifty sandwiches for the party tonight.
4 We might to go out tonight.
5 You won't do well in the test unless you don't study.
6 Ouch! I've been cutting my finger.

/12

FUNCTIONAL LANGUAGE

4 Complete the sentences with the words in the list.

bit | doing | How | matter | news | not | sounds | up

1 A Hi Jack. What's the _____ ?
   B Nothing much. I'm just a _____ upset.
2 A What's _____, Maria? Why are you crying?
   B I'm crying because I'm happy. I won a competition.
   A _____ exciting! I'm really happy for you.
3 A How are you _____ ?
   B Well, _____ great. But I'll be OK, I think.
4 A I've got some _____ ! We're going to get a cat.
   B That _____ great! I'm sure you're really happy.

/8

65

7 FUTURE FUN

OBJECTIVES

FUNCTIONS: checking information; agreeing
GRAMMAR: future forms; question tags; *Nor/Neither / So*
VOCABULARY: future time expressions; arranging a party; phrases with *about*

The WORLD TODAY

22nd July 2042

TRAVEL

Moon hotel to welcome first guests

History will be made today when the Titan Moon Hotel finally opens its doors to welcome the first tourists to the moon. The $36 billion project, which has been delayed for three years, hopes to receive more than 50 guests a week before too long.

The first tourist shuttle leaves for the moon from the London Space Port later this evening. Guests on it include the Internet billionaire Mira Xin and her new husband Bob Latchford. They are spending a three-day honeymoon there.

READING

1 Look at the pictures in the newspaper on these pages. What do the pictures show?

This one shows a building in the future.

2 **SPEAKING** Work in pairs. Think of a current news story for each section of the newspaper.

sport | travel | entertainment
science and technology

Can you think of a science and technology story?

Yes, computers attached to eyeglasses. They're incredible!

3 Look at the pictures again. What do you think the stories are about?

4 Read and check your ideas. What is 'different' about this newspaper?

5 ◆)) 2.06 Read and listen to the stories again. Decide if the sentences are correct or incorrect. Correct the incorrect sentences.

1 They planned to open the Titan Moon Hotel in 2039.
2 Mira Xin has just got married.
3 There are some human actors in *Star Client*.
4 Interflix film producers think actors are too expensive.
5 Shirley Williams lost a foot in a car accident.
6 Doctors thought Shirley's career was over.
7 Dr Miriam Jameson is a scientist.
8 People are already using 3D holograms.

7 FUTURE FUN

ENTERTAINMENT

Actors call for *Star Client* ban

Angry actors are calling on people not to go and see the latest Interflix film *Star Client* because they fear it could be the end of their profession. The film features an entire cast of robots playing human roles. Interflix producers have responded saying that the enormous fees that Hollywood stars are asking for make it impossible for studios to produce films. Maybe actors need not worry too much because early reviews of the film have been terrible. The film opens in the UK on Friday.

SPORT

Shirley's Helsinki Happiness

Doctors have told Shirley Williams that she will be able to compete in the European Championships in Helsinki next month. The 28-year-old boxer had a complete hand transplant after being involved in a car accident in July 2040. Doctors told her that her career was over. But a two-year intensive recovery programme means that she now has the chance to compete again. 'I never thought this day would arrive', she told reporters. 'After Helsinki I'm going to start training for Lima 2044,' she added.

SCIENCE AND TECHNOLOGY

3D holograms a reality, scientists say

Imagine sitting in a business meeting in New York while also sitting in your pyjamas back home in London. According to scientists at the United European University in Zurich, this will be a reality sometime in the near future. Dr Miriam Jameson, head of the science and computing department, held a press conference yesterday to announce a major breakthrough in hologram technology. She promised that two years from now it will be possible to send 3D images of yourself anywhere in the world. Full-body transportation though, she explained, is still just a dream for the future.

THiNK VALUES

Believe in a better future

1 **What kind of future do you think these stories show?**
   - ☺ – a positive future
   - ☺ – not positive or negative
   - ☹ – a negative future

   ☐ Robot films   ☐ 3D holograms
   ☐ Moon hotel   ☐ Miracle boxer

2 **SPEAKING** Work in pairs. Compare your ideas with your partner. Give your reasons.

   > *I think the story about robots acting in films shows a negative future because I don't think that it is a good thing for technology to replace humans.*

3 **SPEAKING** Think of a positive future. What things do you see? Think about these areas.

   technology | medicine | world peace | poverty | sport | weather

   > *No one is hungry.*

GRAMMAR
Future forms

1 Complete the example sentences with the verbs in the list. Check your answers with the stories on pages 66–67. Then match the sentences in Exercise 1 with the rules. Write a–d.

opens | spending | start | will

a The film _____ in the UK on Friday.
b History _____ be made later today.
c I'm going to _____ training for Lima 2044.
d They are _____ a three-day honeymoon there.

RULES: We often use
- the present simple tense to talk about fixed future events. 1 ___
- *be going to* to talk about future plans and intentions. 2 ___
- *will/won't* to make predictions about the future. 3 ___
- the present continuous to talk about future arrangements. 4 ___

2 Complete the sentences. Use the present simple form of the verbs in the list.

arrive | open | finish | start | leave

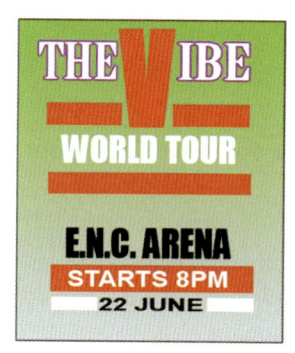

0 The sale *finishes on Friday*.
1 Flight FL098 _____.
2 The concert _____.
3 The train _____.
4 The shop _____.

3 Read the sentences. Mark them P (prediction), I (intention), A (arrangement) or F (fixed event).

1 She won't do very well in her exams. ___
2 They're going to buy a new car soon. ___
3 The match starts at 3 pm. ___
4 He's meeting his mother for lunch on Friday. ___
5 The new zoo opens on Friday. ___
6 One day we'll all live under the sea. ___
7 I'm going to write a novel one day. ___
8 They're having a party on Tuesday. ___

4 Choose the best future form to complete the dialogue.

A ⁰(Are you doing) / Do you do anything on Friday evening?
B Yes, I ¹*'m working* / *'ll work* at the restaurant.
A Oh, what time ²*are you finishing* / *do you finish*?
B The restaurant usually closes at 9 pm and I work until then but there's a party this Friday so I ³*won't* / *don't* finish until at least 10 pm. Why?
A Well I ⁴*'m having* / *'ll have* a party. Lots of people ⁵*come* / *are coming* and I wanted to invite you, too.
B I'd love to come.
A You ⁶*won't be* / *aren't being* too tired?
B No way. It ⁷*is being* / *will be* the perfect way to start the weekend.

> Workbook page 64

VOCABULARY
Future time expressions

1 Complete the time expressions with the words in the list.

from | later | after | time | near | next | next | long

1 the week after _____
2 before too _____
3 in two weeks' _____
4 _____ weekend
5 the day _____ tomorrow
6 _____ today
7 four years _____ now
8 in the _____ future

2 Complete these sentences in your notebook with your own ideas. Think about your family, friends, school, town, country.

Predictions
1 I think _____ in the near future.
2 I think _____ 40 years from now.
3 I think _____ in 20 years' time.

Intentions
4 I _____ the week after next.
5 I _____ next Friday.
6 I _____ before too long.

Arrangements
7 I _____ this weekend.
8 I _____ later today.
9 I _____ tomorrow morning.

> Workbook page 66

7 FUTURE FUN

LISTENING

1 **SPEAKING** You are going to listen to two interviews with people from the future newspaper: boxer Shirley Williams and moon tourist Mira Xin. Compare your questions.
- Student A: Write three questions to ask Shirley.
- Student B: Write three questions to ask Mira.

2 🔊 2.07 Listen to the interviews. Do they ask your questions? What questions do they ask?

3 🔊 2.07 Listen again. Choose the correct picture and put a tick (✓) in the box below it.

1 What is Mira going to do on the moon?

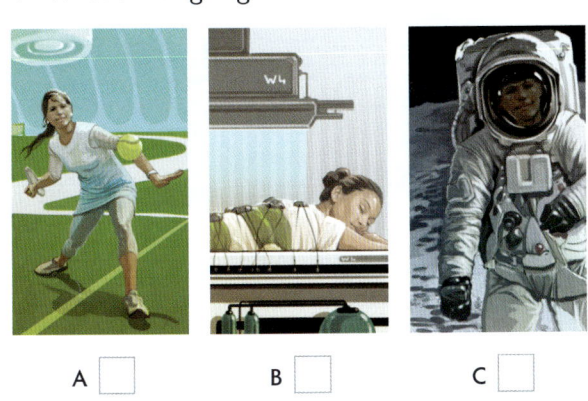

A ☐   B ☐   C ☐

2 What is she taking with her?

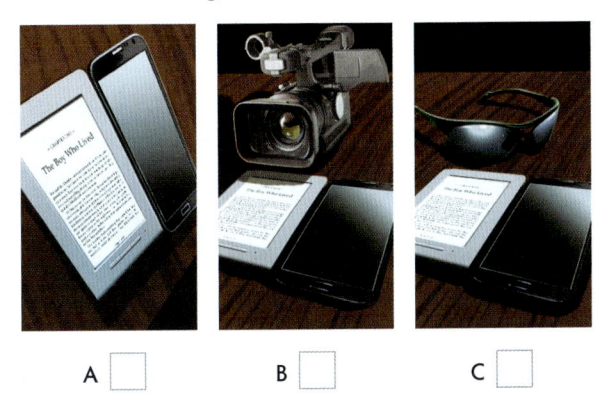

A ☐   B ☐   C ☐

3 What is one of Shirley's plans for the year?

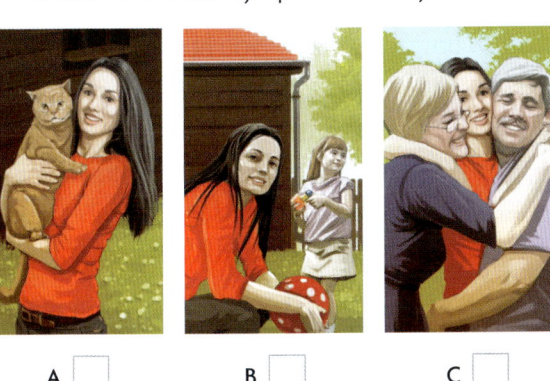

A ☐   B ☐   C ☐

4 What is she going to do?

A ☐   B ☐   C ☐

THiNK SELF-ESTEEM

Personal goals

1 Complete the lists so they are true for you.

Two things I want to do today
1 _____
2 _____

Two things I want to do this week
1 _____
2 _____

Two things I want to do this year
1 _____
2 _____

Two things I want to do in my lifetime
1 _____
2 _____

2 **SPEAKING** Work in pairs. Compare your lists from Exercise 1. Say what things you are going to do.

I really want to finish my school project tonight.

3 **SPEAKING** Discuss how you are going to do the things on your lists.

How are you going to finish your project tonight?

Well, I'm going to start it as soon as I get home. I'm not going to watch any TV.

READING

1. Imagine you are organising a party for your birthday. Put these things in order of importance.

   ☐ food
   ☐ music
   ☐ venue (where you are going to have the party)
   ☐ guests
   ☐ publicity (letting people know about the party)

2. **SPEAKING** Work in pairs. Compare your ideas with a partner.

   > A special venue's not very important. I'll just use my house. Music's very important. You can't have a party without good music.

3. Read the chat room posts quickly. What kind of party are they arranging? Do you think Lucy is a good organiser?

4. Read the posts again. Who is responsible for each area in Exercise 1?

Lucy One week to go, everyone. Just checking in. How's the music going, Fran?

Fran All done. I've hired the DJ. I paid him a deposit. You wanted me to do that, didn't you?

Lucy That's great, Fran. Food – Kev?

Kev All organised. They're delivering the drinks the day after tomorrow.

Lucy But what about the food? You haven't forgotten about that, have you?

Kev All sorted. Jackie and Pete are going to help me on the day.

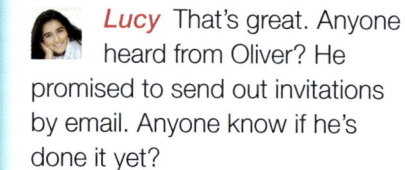

Lucy That's great. Anyone heard from Oliver? He promised to send out invitations by email. Anyone know if he's done it yet?

Oliver What do you mean 'send out invitations'? The party is open to everyone, isn't it? I thought we agreed to put up posters around the school?

Lucy OK, that's a better idea – no need to draw up a guest list and no invitations needed. Just the posters. Lewis, you're doing that, aren't you? Don't forget the theme we've chosen – superheroes.

Lewis I thought that was Vince's job.

Lucy No, I've got you down for posters. Let me know if you can't do it.

Lewis No, that's fine. I'll do it tomorrow. They'll be ready to put up in the afternoon. That should be OK, shouldn't it?

Oliver Yes, and I can help if you want, Lewis.

Kev So can I.

Lewis Great. Can you both come round to my house in the morning?

Oliver Sure, but I won't be able to be there before 11.

Kev Nor will I.

Lewis No problem – see you at about 11 then.

Lucy OK, that's everything, I think. We just need to decorate the room the evening before and we're ready. I'm really going to enjoy this party.

Lewis So am I.

Kev Lucy – is Mr O'Brien OK with it all?

Lucy What?!!?

Kev You've asked Mr O'Brien, haven't you? About having the party, I mean.

Lucy I'm not responsible for that, am I?

Kev Yes, you are, Lucy. I've got the 'to-do' list right here. Check with the headmaster – Lucy. I don't think we can have a party without getting permission from him to use the school hall.

Lucy Neither do I. I'll do it first thing tomorrow. Sorry about that.

7 FUTURE FUN

GRAMMAR
Question tags

1 Complete the sentences. Look at the posts on page 70 and check your answers. Use the sentences in Exercise 1 to complete the rules.

1. You wanted me to do that, _____ you?
2. The party is open to everyone, _____ it?
3. Lewis, you're doing that, _____ you?
4. That should be OK, _____ it?
5. I'm not responsible for that, _____ I?
6. You haven't forgotten about that, _____ you?

> **RULE:** Question tags are short questions which we use to check facts or make conversation.
> - With positive statements, use a ⁰ *negative* question tag.
> - With negative statements, use a ¹_____ question tag.
> - When *be* is used in the statement, repeat it in the question tag. (sentences 2, 3, 5)
> - With modal verbs (*can*, *might*) and most other verb forms, repeat the modal or the auxiliary verb in the question tag. (sentences 4, 6)
> - With present or past simple verbs, use ²_____, *don't*, *does*, ³_____ (present simple) or ⁴_____, *didn't* (past simple). (sentence 1)

2 Complete the questions with tags.

0. She sings beautifully, *doesn't she*?
1. You won't say anything, _____?
2. Debbie didn't phone, _____?
3. You can come to my party, _____?
4. He's Jamie's brother, _____?
5. That meal was delicious, _____?
6. They don't live with you, _____?
7. You've met Liam, _____?
8. You aren't going to university, _____?

Nor/Neither / So

3 Complete the sentences. Then complete the rules.

LUCY	I'm really going to enjoy this party.
LEWIS	So _____ I.
OLIVER	I can help if you want, Lewis.
KEV	So _____ I.
KEV	I don't think we can have a party without getting permission from him.
LUCY	Neither _____ I.
OLIVER	I won't be able to be there before 11.
KEV	Nor _____ I.

> **RULE:** We can use *so* and *nor/neither* to agree with statements.
> - We use ¹_____ to agree with positive statements.
> - We use ²_____ to agree with negative statements.
>
> After *so* and *nor/neither* we repeat the verb used in the statement. If the statement is in the present or past simple, we use *do/did* to agree with it. (See rules on question tags.)

4 Write replies to agree with the statements.

0. I love school. *So do I*.
1. I didn't watch any TV last night.
2. I can't go to the party.
3. I should do my homework.
4. I'm going to bed early tonight.
5. I don't eat meat.
6. I won't be late.
7. I was very upset with Tim.

> Workbook page 65

Pronunciation
Intonation of question tags
Go to page 121.

VOCABULARY
Arranging a party

1 Match verbs with nouns to create a 'to do' list. Use the posts on page 70 to help you.

Verbs	Nouns
send out | organise	permission | room
get | hire | draw up	DJ | food and drinks
decorate	invitations | guest list

Get permission for the party.

2 **SPEAKING** Work in pairs. What order should you do the things on your to do list?

> You should get permission first, shouldn't you?

> Workbook page 66

WRITING
An invitation

You are having a party. Write the invitations. Be sure to say the theme of the party, the date, time and place of the party and also what your guests should bring (or not bring).

71

PHOTOSTORY: episode 4

Weekend plans

1 Look at the photos and answer the questions.
What does Megan want to do on Saturday?
What plans have the others got?

2 🔊 2.10 Now read and listen to the photostory. Check your answers.

1
LUKE Friday morning. I can't wait for the weekend.
OLIVIA Nor can I.
RYAN Only one more day of school to go. Thank goodness! I'm about to go crazy in that classroom.
LUKE I know what you mean.
RYAN And the weather's going to be nice this weekend. I checked the forecast.
MEGAN: So did I. A bit cloudy, but no rain. Let's have a picnic. What do you reckon, Ryan?

2
RYAN I think it's a great idea.
LUKE So do I.
RYAN But I'm going to spend the day with my cousin.
MEGAN Oh, no, that's a shame!
RYAN Hey! There's nothing wrong with my cousin!
MEGAN Oh, come on, Ryan. You know what I mean!

3
MEGAN What about you, Olivia? You haven't got any plans, have you?
OLIVIA Well, actually, yes, I have. Mum promised to take me shopping.
MEGAN Oh. Lucky you.
OLIVIA Yeah, she's going to buy me some new clothes.

4
MEGAN So it's just you and me, Luke.
LUKE Well, Megan, there's a school football match tomorrow morning. And I'm in the team.
MEGAN In other words, you can't come tomorrow either.
LUKE Well, sorry, no. I can't miss the match, can I?
MEGAN Oh, well. Looks like I'm going to be on this bench all alone, then. I'm glad I've got a good book.

7 FUTURE FUN

DEVELOPING SPEAKING

3 Work in pairs. Discuss what happens next in the story. Write down your ideas.

We think that Megan goes shopping with Olivia.

4 ▶ EP4 Watch to find out how the story continues.

5 Answer the questions.
1. Why doesn't Ryan go to his cousin's house?
2. Why doesn't Luke play football?
3. Why doesn't Olivia go shopping?

PHRASES FOR FLUENCY

1 Find the expressions 1–6 in the story. Who says them? How do you say them in your language?

1. Thank goodness.
2. What do you reckon?
3. That's a shame.
4. There's nothing wrong with …
5. Lucky you.
6. In other words, …

2 Complete the conversations. Use the expressions in Exercise 1.

1. **A** My parents just won a holiday in a competition.
   B Wow! _____!
   A The holiday is for two people, so I can't go.
   B Oh. _____.
2. **A** How's Ben? Any news?
   B Yes. He's OK. His arm's not broken. _____.
   A _____, it's not as serious as we thought.
3. **A** Look at that guy's clothes. They're horrible! _____?
   B Well, I don't like them much. But I don't think you should be so critical.
   A Hey! _____ saying what you think!

WordWise
Phrases with *about*

1 Complete the sentences from the unit so far with a phrase in the list.

sorry about | about eleven | about you
forgotten about | about to

1. No problem – see you _____ then.
2. What about the food? You haven't _____ that, have you?
3. I'll do it first thing tomorrow. _____ that.
4. I'm _____ go crazy in that classroom.
5. What _____, Olivia?

2 Match the questions and answers.

1. How tall is Jack?
2. You haven't tidied up!
3. I love this music. What about you?
4. Has your sister left school now?
5. Why weren't you at the party?

a. Yes. She's about to go to university.
b. About 1 metre 65, I think.
c. I forgot about it. I'm really angry with myself!
d. Yes, it's not bad.
e. Oh, sorry about that.

3 Complete the sentences so they are true for you. Then compare with a partner.

1. I usually get up about …
2. Once, I forgot about …
3. I've got a friend who is about to …

Workbook page 66

FUNCTIONS
Agreeing

1 Match the sentences and the replies from *Weekend plans*.

1. I can't wait for the weekend.
2. I checked the forecast.
3. I think it's a great idea.
4. I'm happy you're here.
5. I haven't got anything to do all day.
6. I didn't want to spoil the surprise.

a. So did I.
b. So am I.
c. Neither have I.
d. Neither did I.
e. Nor can I.
f. So do I.

2 Complete the left-hand column with true information about you.

Tonight I'm going to …	and so is _____ .
I'm not going to …	nor is _____ .
Yesterday I …	and so did _____ .
Yesterday I didn't …	nor did _____ .
I really like …	and so does _____ .
I don't like …	nor does _____ .

3 Walk about the classroom and find people who agree with you. Complete the chart with their names.

73

8 SCIENCE COUNTS

OBJECTIVES

FUNCTIONS: talking about past habits; talking about imaginary situations; talking about scientific discoveries
GRAMMAR: past simple vs. past continuous (review); *used to*; second conditional; *I wish*
VOCABULARY: direction and movement; science

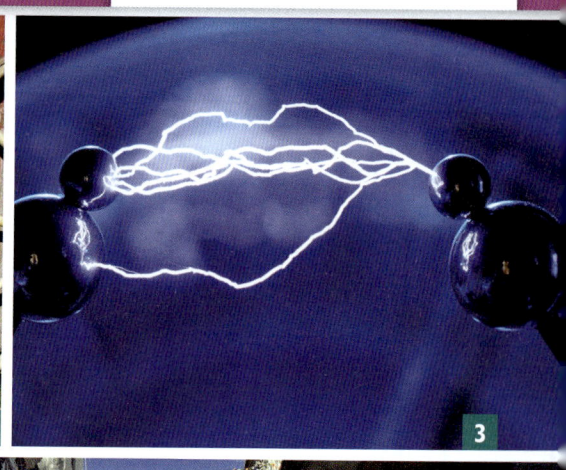

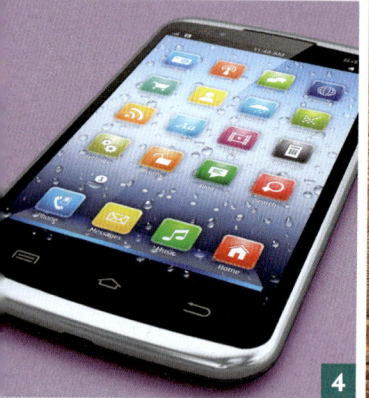

READING

1 **Look at the pictures. Say what each one shows.**

> Picture 3 is electricity.

2 **SPEAKING** Work in pairs. Answer the questions.
  1 Why are the things in Exercise 1 important?
  2 What was life like for people before they had these things?

> Before people had fire, they couldn't cook meat. And they were cold in winter.

3 **SPEAKING** Work in pairs or small groups. Discuss the questions.
  1 Electricity and fire are *discoveries*. The other things are *inventions*. What's the difference?
  2 Which of the six things above do you think is the most important? Why?
  3 Can you think of other discoveries or inventions that changed how people live?

4 **Look at the pictures on page 75.**
  1 Who are the people, do you think?
  2 What do you think this blog is about?

5 🔊 **2.11** Read and listen to the blog and check your ideas.

6 **Read the blog again. Answer the questions.**
  1 What did Newton think about when he saw the apple fall to the ground?
  2 What did Archimedes see when he got out of the bath?
  3 Why did he shout 'Eureka'?
  4 Why are these discoveries not complete accidents?

74

8 SCIENCE COUNTS

MIKE HORNBY'S VERY INTERESTING BLOG PAGE

Why aren't people more interested in science?

Welcome to my blog, where I write about the things that really interest me! This week I want to talk a bit about science, scientists and science stories.

Let's start with Newton. We all know the story, don't we? Back in about 1666, Isaac Newton was visiting his mother one day and was walking around in her garden. He sat down under an apple tree and started thinking. (Newton was always thinking about something, that's what scientists do.) So, he was sitting and thinking when an apple fell out of the tree and hit the ground beside him. (Some people say the apple fell on his head, but who knows?) And Newton thought about why things fall down and not up or sideways. And he got the idea of gravity.

Nice story, isn't it? Only it's probably not true. Or, at least, we've got no way of knowing if it's true. It's a bit like Archimedes and the bath. You don't know that one?

OK, so a Greek mathematician was sitting in his bath one day, more than two thousand years ago, and while he was getting out, he noticed that the water went down in the bath. So he got back in, and the water went back up. 'Now I understand!' shouted Archimedes – actually, he shouted 'Eureka!' because he was Greek, not English. He saw that the level of the water in the bath was directly related to exactly how much of his body was in the water, that this relationship was constant – it never changed! Some people say that he was so happy about his discovery that he ran out into the street without putting his clothes on. No, that probably didn't happen either, but he had a good reason to be happy. This was a very important moment in our understanding of maths and physics.

The stories are hard to believe. But the important thing is that Archimedes and Newton really did exist, and they really did come up with those important ideas. Newton worked out that if the Earth's gravity has an effect on the movement of an apple, then it probably has an effect on the movement of the moon, too – and all kinds of new ideas and discoveries came from that.

And you might say that these discoveries were accidents, and in a way they were – but not complete accidents. They needed people like Newton and Archimedes to do the thinking. Scientists and mathematicians do a lot of thinking and because of that, our world is the way it is.

THiNK VALUES

How science helps people

1 **Choose the sentence that you think best says what the blog is about.**
   1 Some important things happen by accident.
   2 You shouldn't believe everything you read about science.
   3 Scientists should be more famous than they are.
   4 It's important to know something about science.

2 **SPEAKING** Compare your ideas with others in the class.

3 **SPEAKING** Here are four things that science has given us. Write down three more. Then, with your partner(s), discuss the question: How do these things help us every day?

the Internet   the telephone   medicines   the fridge

75

GRAMMAR
Past simple vs. past continuous (review)

1 **Complete the sentences from the text with the words in the list. Then complete the rules with** *past simple*, *past continuous*, *when* **and** *while*.

fell | sitting | went | hit | thinking getting | noticed

1. Newton was _____ and _____ when an apple _____ out of the tree and _____ the ground.
2. While Archimedes was _____ out of the bath, he _____ that the water _____ down.

RULE: We use
- the ¹_____ for an action that happened at a particular moment in the past. We often use ²_____ with this tense.
- the ³_____ for a background action or to describe a situation over a period of time in the past. We often use ⁴_____ with this tense.

Remember that some verbs can't be used in the continuous form.

2 **Complete the sentences with the correct past tense form of the verbs.**

0. While Benjamin Franklin *was watching* a thunderstorm, he *got* some ideas about electricity. (watch / get)
1. We _____ an experiment at school when a fire _____ . (do / start)
2. They _____ for lunch because they _____ enough time. (not stop / have)
3. The electricity _____ off at home while I _____ my homework. (go / do)
4. I _____ a great science site while I _____ the net. (discover / surf)
5. Who _____ you _____ to when I _____ you in town yesterday? (talk / see)
6. When the scientist _____ the answer to the problem, she _____ very famous. (find / become)

3 **Sally saw an incident in her town centre. Complete her statement to the police with the past simple or past continuous form of the verbs in the list. Sometimes more than one verb is possible.**

~~buy~~ | ~~sit~~ | read | see | walk | stand | hit not stop | do | cycle | ride | go | knock

Last Saturday morning I ⁰ *bought* a magazine, and I ⁰ *sat* down on a bench in the town centre to read it. People ¹_____ about and ²_____ their shopping. There was a group of four people near me – they ³_____ together and laughing. Then I ⁴_____ a boy, about 16 years old. He ⁵_____ his bike down the street. He ⁶_____ very fast. Suddenly, he had to change direction because there was an old lady in front of him, and he ⁷_____ right into the group of people. His bike ⁸_____ a man and ⁹_____ him over. And the boy ¹⁰_____ . He just cycled away!

➡ Workbook page 72

VOCABULARY
Direction and movement

1 **Complete the sentence.**

Newton thought about why things fall ¹_____ and not ²_____.

2 **Match the phrases with the pictures.**
1. It's coming **towards** her.
2. It's running **away from** her.
3. They're running **around** the tree.
4. She's leaning **backwards**.
5. She's leaning **forwards**.
6. He's walking **up and down** the room.

A ☐   B ☐   C ☐
D ☐   E ☐   F ☐

LOOK! *Forwards* and *backwards* are the only words here that are never followed by an object.

The words *towards* and *away from* always have an object after them.

3 **Which way(s) can these things move?**
1. a car
2. a plane
3. a helicopter
4. a lion in a cage

➡ Workbook page 74

8 SCIENCE COUNTS

LISTENING

1 Look at the pictures. In which picture can you see …:

1. apple seeds?
2. the moon?
3. a plug in a socket?
4. a hose?

2 🔊 2.12 Listen to a class discussion. You will hear four stories about things children didn't understand. Number the pictures in the order you hear the stories.

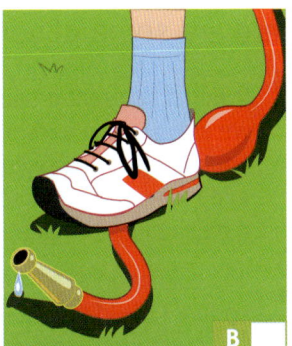

3 🔊 2.12 Listen again. Answer the questions.

1. When the teacher was a girl, why did she think she might get ill during the night?
2. Why did Sarah use to look at the moon for hours?
3. Why did Sarah laugh at the moon?
4. Why didn't Alex's grandfather use to step on wires?
5. Why did Martin's family eat lots of apples?
6. Why was Martin afraid to eat apple seeds?

GRAMMAR
used to

1 Complete these sentences with the words in the list. Then choose the correct words to complete the rule.

do | be | laugh | plug | eat

1. Every night I **used to** _____ something into all the electrical sockets.
2. **Did** you really **use to** _____ that, Miss?
3. I **used to** _____ at the moon and call it names.
4. He **used to** _____ scared of standing on a wire.
5. I **didn't use to** _____ the seeds.

RULE: We can use *used to* + verb to talk about things that happened regularly in the past but not any more.
- In the positive, we say ¹*used / use to* + verb.
- In the negative, we say *didn't* ²*used / use to* + verb
- For questions, we say *Did* [you] ³*used / use to* + verb

2 Complete the sentences. Use the correct form of *used to* and the present simple.

0. That shop <u>used to be</u> (be) a book shop, but now it <u>sells</u> (sell) clothes.
1. He _____ (be) my friend, but we really _____ (not know) each other any more.
2. When we were younger, we _____ (not listen) to country music, but now we _____ (not listen) to anything else.
3. I really _____ (not like) pizza now, but it _____ (be) my favourite food.
4. We _____ (go) to Greece for our holidays, but now we _____ (prefer) Spain.
5. My sister _____ (believe) there were monsters under her bed.
6. I _____ (not care) about science, but now I _____ (think) it's really interesting.
7. When you were small, _____ you _____ (have) an imaginary friend?

Pronunciation
The /juː/ sound
Turn to page 121. 🔊

Workbook page 72

FUNCTIONS
Talking about past habits

1 Think about life when you were much younger. Write five things that you or others used to do or believe.

2 **SPEAKING** Work in small groups. Talk about the things you wrote. Who has the funniest story?

When I was little I used to think that there was a person inside the post box who took the letters.

My brother and I used to hide in my sister's closet and then jump out and scare her when she opened the door.

READING

1 **SPEAKING** Think of something that doesn't exist yet but that you would like to have or to see. Compare your ideas with a partner.

> I'd like to have a motorbike that can also fly.

> I'd like to see a machine that can take you anywhere in the world in seconds.

2 A web forum asked readers to do the same task as Exercise 1. Look at the pictures. What things do you think the forum readers suggested?

3 Read the forum. Check your answers to Exercise 2.

4 Read the forum again. Then write the names of the people described in these statements.

- 0 This person thinks about our planet. *Charlie*
- 1 This person might be a bit lazy. _____
- 2 This person worries about sick people. _____
- 3 This person wants more time. _____
- 4 This person wants to go back in time. _____

TRAIN TO THiNK

Using criteria

1 Here are the five ideas from the forum. Put them in order 1–5: 1 = the most useful, 5 = the least useful.

- [ ] a a fuel that doesn't pollute
- [ ] b a time machine
- [ ] c a cure for malaria
- [ ] d a machine to do homework
- [ ] e a pill to sleep less

2 **SPEAKING** Compare your ideas with a partner.

3 You put the five things in order following a criterion – how useful is the idea? Here are two more criteria. Can you think of others?

- How *possible* is it?
- How *important* is it?
- How _____ is it?
- How _____ is it?

4 Choose one of the criteria in Exercise 3 and order the things in Exercise 1 again. Then compare your ideas with other students.

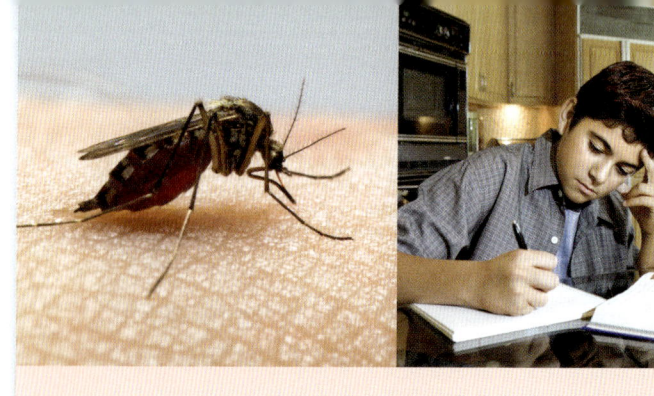

We asked you, our readers:
'What scientific advance or discovery would you like to see in the near future?'
Here are some of your answers.

1   It would be great if there was some kind of petrol we could use in cars that didn't produce any pollution. I guess there are scientists right now trying to do that, and I hope they succeed, because the world would be a much cleaner place, wouldn't it? **Charlie**

2   If I could choose anything, I'd go for a time machine so that I could go back and do some things differently. Of course that's impossible – but wouldn't it be great if it was possible? I wish I could go back in time to when I was a kid and not say some of the things that I really did say! **Hannah**

3   Well, of course, the best things are cures for really bad diseases. Everyone thinks about cancer, and of course it's terrible, but a lot of scientists are also working very hard to stop malaria – another terrible disease that affects millions of people all over the world. So if they found a cure for malaria, or a way of completely preventing it, life would be easier in so many places. **Bruna**

4   I wish there was a machine that did homework! Wouldn't that be fantastic? But I guess teachers wouldn't be very happy. **Georgina**

5   I think it would be great if they invented a pill or something so that you only had to sleep for one or two hours every day. Then we'd all have much more time to do things and to enjoy ourselves. Life would be better, I think, and everyone would do a lot more with their lives. **Morris**

8 SCIENCE COUNTS

GRAMMAR
Second conditional

1 **Complete these sentences with the phrases in the list. Are the sentences about real or imagined situations? Find more examples of the second conditional in the web forum and underline them.**

would be | would go for | wouldn't it be
was | found | could

1 If they _____ a cure for malaria, life _____ easier in so many places.
2 If I _____ choose anything, I _____ a time machine.
3 _____ great if it _____ possible?

2 **Now complete the rule.**

> **RULE:** We use the second conditional to talk about the consequences of an unreal present action or ¹ *a probable / an improbable* future action.
> - Condition clause: *if* + ²_____ simple.
> - Result clause: ³_____ / *wouldn't* (*would not*) + verb.
>
> The condition clause can come before or after the result clause.

3 **Circle the correct words.**

0 If I (had) / would have a bit more time, I went / (would go) and see my friends tonight.
1 They would learn / learned more if they would listen / listened more carefully.
2 If my school would be / was a long way from home, I would have / had to take a bus.
3 He lent / would lend you his tablet if you asked / would ask him nicely.
4 If he was / would be really ill, he stay / would stay in bed.
5 I gave / would give you her address if I knew / would know it myself.

4 **Complete the sentences with the correct form of the verbs.**

0 I think it *'d be* (be) a great party if the food *was* (be) better.
1 Who _____ you _____ (talk) to if you _____ (have) a really serious problem?
2 She _____ (like) you if you _____ (be) nicer to her.
3 If his father _____ (not make) him tidy his room, he _____ (not do) it.
4 If you _____ (can) have any present you want, what _____ you _____ (choose)?

I wish

5 **Read the sentences. How are they alike?**

1 I wish I could go back to when I was a kid.
2 I wish there was a machine that did homework.

6 **Complete the sentences with the correct verb form.**

0 The bus isn't here. I wish the bus *was* here.
1 We aren't a good team. I wish we _____ a better team.
2 I can't go home. I wish I _____ go home.
3 It's raining. I wish it _____ raining.
4 They are making so much noise! I wish they _____ so much noise!

7 **SPEAKING** Work in pairs. Which person in the pictures is thinking which thing from Exercise 6? (More than one answer is possible.)

Workbook page 73

VOCABULARY
Science

1 **Match the words with the definitions.**

1	a cure	a	to study something
2	to discover	b	someone who works in an area of science
3	an experiment	c	a room for scientific work
4	to invent	d	something that makes a sick person well again
5	a laboratory	e	to find something new
6	a machine	f	a test to see if something works or is true
7	to do research	g	to make something new
8	a scientist	h	a piece of equipment that does a specific kind of work

2 **SPEAKING** Look back at Reading Exercise 1 on page 78.

1 What do you think are the three best ideas?
2 Write them again, using either *I wish …* or the second conditional.

3 **SPEAKING** In class, compare everyone's ideas, and vote for the best ones.

Workbook page 74

Culture

1 Look at the photos. What things can you see in each one?

2 🔊 2.15 Read and listen to the article about five scientists. Number the photos 1–5.

Great scientists

1 Galileo (Italy, 1564–1642)

Galileo – his full name was Galileo Galilei – is sometimes called 'the father of modern science'. He was a scientist, mathematician and astronomer (someone who looks at the stars and planets). When he was alive, telescopes were still quite **basic**, and he made many improvements to them.

His best-known **achievement** was to show that the Earth moves around the sun, and not the sun around the Earth (although he was not the first man to have the idea).

2 Louis Pasteur (France, 1822–1895)

Louis Pasteur was one of the people who started the area of science that we now call microbiology. He did many things during his life, but he is remembered mostly because of the work that he did with milk. When milk is about two days old, it starts to get bacteria (very small things that carry disease), and this makes it dangerous to drink – people can get diseases. Pasteur developed a way to **prevent** this happening. The process is called 'pasteurisation'.

3 Karl Landsteiner (Austria, 1868–1943)

Landsteiner worked in Vienna on many scientific things. Together with a man called Erwin Popper, he helped to **identify** the virus that causes a disease called polio.

But even more importantly, in 1901 he discovered the three main blood groups – A, B and O – and showed that it is possible to transfer blood from one person to another person. This led to the first ever blood transfusion in 1907, in New York.

4 Francis Crick (Britain, 1916–2004) and James Watson (USA, born 1928)

In 1953, in Cambridge, UK, Crick and Watson told the world that they had found 'the secret of life'. The secret is the **structure** of DNA, the material that makes genes, the things we get from our parents that control how we grow. Their discovery meant that we now know much, much more about the human body. And with that knowledge, there have been **enormous** improvements in medicine and medical research, as well as in historical research and solving crimes.

5 Jane Goodall (Britain, born 1934)

Jane Goodall is a scientist who has studied primates, especially chimpanzees, her whole life. She has studied their family groups, their use of **tools** and their emotions. Her work has made it clear that chimpanzees and other primates (gorillas, for example) are not as different from people as we used to think. Goodall has shown the world that we need to **treat** the animals around us with respect and protect them.

8 SCIENCE COUNTS

3 Read the article again and write the names of the scientists.

Which scientist (or scientists) …
1 … is/are still alive?
2 … looked at stars?
3 … worked with animals?
4 … did work that helped medicine?
5 … started a new science?
6 … invented something to stop diseases?
7 … improved a piece of equipment?
8 … did work that helped historians and detectives?

4 SPEAKING Discuss the questions.
a Which of the scientists do you think is the most important? Why? Share your ideas with the class.
b There is only one woman here. Why do you think this is?

5 SPEAKING Match the words in bold in the article with their meanings. Write the words.

0 the way that the parts of something are organized
   structure
1 say who or what someone or something is _____
2 very, very big or important _____
3 simple, not complicated _____
4 something very good and difficult that you do _____
5 stop, not allow _____
6 to behave towards people or things in a certain way _____
7 things you use with your hands to do jobs _____

WRITING
A blog entry

1 Ellen wrote a blog entry with the title, 'A world without television'. Read what she wrote and answer the questions.
a What did people do before they had television?
b What does Ellen think life would be like without TV?

2 Look at Ellen's blog entry again.
1 In which paragraph does Ellen use *used to*? In which does she use the second conditional?
2 Match the paragraphs with these headings:
   A Imagine life without television
   B Life before television

3 You are going to write a blog entry like Ellen's. Choose one of these pieces of technology, or another one if you prefer:
   – mobile phones   – tablets
   – the Internet   – calculators

4 Make notes for your blog entry.

Paragraph 1: what life was like / what people did before the piece of technology was invented
_____
_____
_____

Paragraph 2: what life would be like now without the piece of technology
_____
_____
_____

5 Write your blog entry. Write 120–180 words altogether.

Ellen's blog

A world without television

[1] It isn't easy to imagine life without television, but people only started to have television at home about sixty years ago. So a lot of people who are alive today lived without it in the past. Before television, people used to read in the evening, or listen to the radio. I read once that families used to get together and sing songs or tell each other stories. I think it was probably a bit boring but perhaps people enjoyed it.

[2] If we didn't have television these days, I think things would be OK. I mean, we would still have films and the Internet, wouldn't we? We would get all the information and entertainment we need there, and in fact many people already do. I know a lot of people who don't watch television at all, they watch sport and things by streaming them. But of course, they're using TV programmes when they do that – so maybe a world without TV wouldn't be such a good idea!

CAMBRIDGE ENGLISH: Preliminary

THiNK EXAMS

READING

Part 1: Three-option multiple choice
Workbook page 71

1 Look at the text in each question. What does it say? Choose the correct letter A, B or C.

0 RED BUTTON STOPS THE ESCALATOR. ONLY USE IN CASE OF EMERGENCY
- A Press the red button if you want to get on the escalator.
- **B** Don't press the red button unless there is a serious problem.
- C Only shop staff can press the red button.

1 Subject: Hi Claudia - I want to start French lessons. You said John Gray teaches French. Have you got his phone number? best Anna

Anna
- A wants Claudia to pass on a message to John Gray.
- B wants to talk to John Gray.
- C wishes she could start French lessons.

2 PHOTOGRAPHY FOR BEGINNERS
5-week course starts Tuesday 5th Oct.
There are still a few places.
BOOK WITH STEVE
- A The photography course is already full.
- B Talk to Steve if you are interested in learning how to take photographs.
- C The photography course finishes at the end of October.

3 The recent rain has made the school fields very wet and we might need to move the school sports day from Saturday to Sunday. Please see this notice board for further information.
- A The sports day will now take place on Sunday.
- B The weather will be bad this weekend.
- C There is a chance the sports day will still take place on Saturday.

4 Jemma – would it be OK if you didn't use any of the eggs? I need them to make a cake when I get back from work. Thanks Jim PS Help yourself to the soup – it's delicious.

Jemma can
- A eat the soup but not the eggs.
- B eat the soup and some of the eggs.
- C have some cake when Jim gets back from work.

5 Really sorry to miss your party. Hope it's fun. Work is no fun at all!

Fin
- A wishes he could go to Ashley's party.
- B is going to be late for the party.
- C thinks that work is as fun as the party.

WRITING

Part 1: Sentence transformations
Workbook page 17

2 Here are some sentences about science. For each question, complete the second sentence so that it means the same as the first. Use no more than three words.

0 My dad's worked as a scientist for 20 years.
My dad started working as a scientist _20 years ago_ .

1 I really don't understand physics. I would like to understand it.
I wish _____ physics.

2 I'm quite sure he doesn't like science.
He really doesn't like science, _____ ?

3 Before Mr O'Brian was our teacher, I didn't like science much.
I _____ like science before Mr O'Brian became our teacher.

4 I always fail biology tests because I don't understand things.
If I understood things, I _____ biology tests.

5 I don't enjoy science fiction, and Jim doesn't enjoy science fiction.
I don't enjoy science fiction, and _____ Jim.

TEST YOURSELF

UNITS 7 & 8

VOCABULARY

1 Complete the sentences with the words in the list. There are two extra words.

experiment | up and down | away | towards | hire | near
research | long | cure | next | later | draw up

1. Sorry, I can't come and see you for a couple of weeks – but how about the week after _____ ?
2. I got scared when the dog started running _____ me.
3. I'm going to do an _____ to see if my idea works.
4. I think we should _____ a list of all the things we've got to do.
5. I can't talk to you right now. Could you please phone me back _____ today.
6. It's my brother's 18th birthday next week, and we're going to _____ a band to play at the party.
7. She's got a serious disease, and the doctor says there's no _____ for it.
8. I'm going to do some _____ on the Internet before I write my essay.
9. She was very late! I got a bit nervous and started walking _____ outside the cinema.
10. We're hoping to buy a bigger flat in the _____ future.

/10

GRAMMAR

2 Complete the sentences. Put the verbs in brackets into the correct form or write the missing word(s) in the space.

1. I missed the bus, so I _____ (walk) home.
2. This computer's really fast, _____ ?
3. I saw Jack while I _____ (walk) in town yesterday.
4. A I really don't like him.
   B _____ do I.
5. Your computer's got lots of memory, _____ ?
6. A I hate sport.
   B _____ do I.

3 Find and correct the mistake in each sentence.

1. When I was a kid, I used to playing with toy cars.
2. If you would work harder, you would do better at school.
3. When you phoned me, I had dinner.
4. The world was a happier place if people smiled more.
5. James never listens to pop music, and so do I.
6. I wish this homework isn't so difficult!

/12

FUNCTIONAL LANGUAGE

4 Write the missing words.

1. A I can't _____ for the Rihanna concert.
   B _____ can I! It's going to be fantastic.
2. A I _____ to love that programme when I was a kid.
   B So _____ I. I thought it was great.
3. A I _____ it wasn't raining.
   B _____ do I. I want to go for a walk!
4. A Where's Alex? I wish he _____ here.
   B So _____ I. Parties are always better with Alex!

/8

MY SCORE /30

22 – 30
10 – 21
0 – 9

9 WHAT A JOB!

OBJECTIVES

FUNCTIONS: accepting and refusing invitations
GRAMMAR: the passive (present simple, past simple, present continuous, present perfect)
VOCABULARY: jobs; work as / in / for; work vs. job; time expressions with *in*

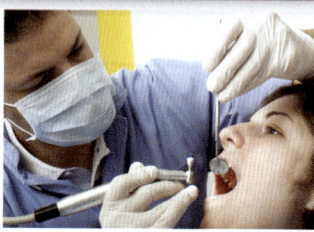

READING

1 What jobs do you see in the photos on this page? What other jobs can you name in English? With a partner, write down as many as you can.

2 Which of the jobs you thought of in Exercise 1 …
   1 sometimes involves work in the evening or at night?
   2 needs a lot of training?
   3 involves work at weekends?
   4 is well paid?
   5 gets a lot of holidays?
   6 can be dangerous?

3 **SPEAKING** Compare your ideas from Exercises 1 and 2 with others in the class.

4 Look at the photographs on page 85. What jobs do you think the people have?

5 🔊 2.16 Look at the sentences below about different jobs. Read and listen to the article and decide if each sentence is correct or incorrect. If it is correct, mark it A. If it is incorrect, mark it B.
   1 Children all over Britain eat Swizell's sweets.
   2 All the sweets that Harry tests are good.
   3 Harry tests the sweets at the factory.
   4 Ben Southall had an interview for his job.
   5 Ben lived alone in the villa.
   6 Ben didn't do his job very well.
   7 Roisin worked for a month for £1,000.
   8 Roisin worked for a hotel.
   9 Roisin sometimes spent ten hours in a test bed.

THINK VALUES

What's important in a job?

1 What do you think about Harry, Ben and Roisin's jobs? Tick the boxes.

	Harry	Ben	Roisin
1 This job is a waste of time.	☐	☐	☐
2 This job sounds fun.	☐	☐	☐
3 This job doesn't help anyone.	☐	☐	☐
4 This job is paid too much money.	☐	☐	☐
5 I would like to have this job.	☐	☐	☐

2 **SPEAKING** Compare your ideas with others in the class.

3 Think of a job you might like to do in the future and write it down. Look at values a–f below. Rank each one 1–6 (1 = low, 6 = high) for your job.

Job:

Value	Score
a You can make a lot of money.	
b You might become famous.	
c It helps people.	
d It's fun to do.	
e It gives you lots of free time.	
f It's creative.	

4 **SPEAKING** Talk to others in your class. Compare your job and values with theirs.

9 WHAT A JOB!

Dream JOBS

Have you ever imagined the perfect job?
What would you choose?
Here are three that would be on our list!

The sweetest job

Swizell's is a company in Britain that makes sweets. The sweets are made in the company's factory near Manchester in the north of England, and they're eaten by kids all over the country. Harry Willsher is one of the company's employees, but he's only 12 years old! His job is probably the best job in the factory – he's the company's official sweet tester.

When a new sweet is invented, it's made in a special department in the factory – all very secret. Then, the new sweet is sent to Harry's house for him to test. He eats it, writes a report about it and sends his report to the factory. And then a decision is made about whether to make the sweet or not.

Is Harry paid for the job? Well, no, he isn't paid because he's too young to work for money. But he gets free sweets!

Harry says: 'When I started the job, I felt like I was in the book Charlie and the Chocolate Factory!' Harry has got a special uniform and business cards. He's got a really sweet job, you might say!

Desert Island Blogger

Would you like to look after an island in the Pacific Ocean? Almost 35,000 people applied for the job, but Ben Southall got it. How was the winner chosen? Well, after Ben showed that he was good at blogging and swimming, there was an interview. He was asked lots of questions to see if he had the right kind of personality for the job. And he did!

So what did Ben have to do in this job? It was hard work! He had to live on his own in a 3-bedroom villa (with a swimming pool) on Hamilton Island and spend every day swimming, exploring and relaxing. Then he had to write a blog to promote the area.

Ben was paid $111,000 for six months' work. The people he worked for liked his work very much. After he finished on Hamilton Island, he became Tourism Ambassador for the state of Queensland, Australia.

Sleeping on the job

Usually, sleeping on the job is a big problem for an employee – if you fall asleep, you'll be fired! But Roisin Madigan, from Birmingham, UK, was paid to sleep on the job. She tested luxury beds.

Roisin was paid £1,000 to sleep in designer beds every day for a month. A company that makes beds for luxury hotels wanted to know more about what makes 'a good night's sleep'. Roisin was selected to spend up to eight hours a day in a bed and then write about it. Over 600 people applied for the job, but they weren't chosen, of course – it was only Roisin who got to sleep on the job!

GRAMMAR
The passive: present simple and past simple

1 Complete the sentences from the article on page 85. Then choose the correct options to complete the rules about the passive.

1 The sweets _____ in the company's factory.
2 _____ Harry _____ for the job?
3 No, he _____ because he's too young.
4 How _____ the winner _____ ?
5 He _____ lots of questions.
6 Over 600 people applied for the job, but they _____ , of course.

> **RULE:** Form the passive with the verb ¹*to be / to have* + the past participle of the main verb.
> We use the passive when
> - it ²*is / isn't* important who does or did the action.
> - we ³*want / don't want* to focus on the action and not the person doing it.
> - we ⁴*know / don't know* who does or did the action.

2 Complete the sentences with the present simple passive or past simple passive form of the verbs.

0 Every year, hundreds of films *are made* (make) in Hollywood.
1 It was interesting work, but she _____ (not pay) very much money.
2 Tigers _____ (not find) in Africa.
3 This novel _____ (write) a hundred years ago.
4 Lots of new websites _____ (design) especially for small children.
5 When _____ the Mona Lisa _____ (paint)?
6 In the USA, the president _____ (choose) every four years.
7 _____ you _____ (ask) to help with the party?
8 Why _____ permission _____ (not give) for the party?

3 How many passive sentences can you make? (Your sentences can be positive or negative.)

Millions of pizzas	build	fifty years ago
The World Cup	buy	every day
How many emails	eat	last night
Our house	discover	every day
America	make	in 1492
This email	play	in China
My computer	send	to me by mistake
How many songs	use	every four years
This book	write	two years ago

▶ Workbook page 82

VOCABULARY
Jobs

1 Read the essay. Which jobs does the writer talk about?

> My first job was as a waiter. I did it when I first left school, just **to earn** money. It was fun, really, but it was very hard work. I had **to work long hours** and of course I was always on my feet! It wasn't very **challenging** – I had to remember the customers' orders, but that was all, really. And I didn't **get paid holidays**, so that wasn't good.
>
> So after about five months I **gave in my notice** and got a job as a shop assistant in a bookstore. I really enjoyed that because I like books and I like talking to people about them. I was very good at the job, and after a few months I was **promoted** to store manager. That was great! I got **on-the-job training** about management and things, and I was happy because I was **starting a career** – well, I thought I was. After two years, the bookstore closed because there wasn't enough business.
>
> Now I've got a few more years' experience, and I work as a management consultant. **The pay** is fantastic and the work is quite interesting. I guess you can say I'm **successful**. But you know what? Sometimes I miss being a waiter and just having jokes with the customers!

2 Match the expressions in bold with their definitions. Write the words.

0 the money you get for doing a job *the pay*
1 to get money for doing a job _____
2 given a higher position _____
3 beginning a job (or series of jobs) that you might do for life _____
4 achieving a lot, and/or making a lot of money _____
5 be paid for the weeks that you don't work _____
6 said you didn't want a job any more _____
7 to work many hours every day _____
8 a way of learning to do a job at the same time that you do it _____
9 difficult in a way that tests your abilities _____

Pronunciation
/tʃ/ and /dʒ/ consonant sounds
Go to page 121.

9 WHAT A JOB!

3 SPEAKING
Look at these jobs. Which sentences can be used to describe each job? (There's often more than one possibility.) Compare your ideas with others in your class.

1. You have to work long hours.
2. The pay can be excellent.
3. If you're good at the job, you might be promoted.
4. It's a very good career.
5. It's not challenging at all.
6. The only reason to do this job is to earn money.
7. If you're successful in this job, you could be famous.
8. You can do this job with on-the-job training.

Workbook page 84

LISTENING

1
Look at the pictures of three people who are disabled. Match these words to the pictures.

1 blind   2 deaf   3 in a wheelchair

2 SPEAKING
Here are some jobs. Do you think that people with the disabilities in Exercise 1 can do all of these jobs? Why or why not?

1 teacher   4 pilot
2 actor   5 shop assistant
3 musician   6 taxi driver

I think a person in a wheelchair can be a teacher, but I'm not sure if a deaf person can be a teacher.

3 ◉ 2.19
Listen to a programme with a woman called Marina Stuart. Choose the correct options.

1 Marina is …
   a deaf.   b blind.   c in a wheelchair.

2 Marina works as …
   a an actor.
   b a piano teacher.
   c an actor and a piano teacher.

4 ◉ 2.19
Listen again and answer the questions.

1 What happened to Marina when she was 18?
2 What were the teachers like at her school?
3 Why didn't she leave the job that she hated?
4 Who did Marina meet by accident?
5 How many of the films she was in won an award?
6 Why does Marina think she has been successful?

THiNK SELF-ESTEEM

I'd rather be …

1
Think about possible jobs and the characteristics connected to them. For each group of words (1–5), tick the job you would rather have or the type of person you would rather be.

I would rather be …

1	an actor		a musician		a dancer
2	a waiter		a cleaner		a gardener
3	a teacher		a firefighter		a police officer
4	rich		famous		clever
5	successful		helpful		kind

2 SPEAKING
Work in small groups. Compare your answers and say why you chose them.

I'd rather be an actor because I don't like music very much.

I'd rather be a waiter because then you can talk to people all day.

READING

1 Look at the photographs. Which one shows …

1 something to do with telephones?
2 something to do with books?
3 something to do with lights?
4 something to do with lifts?

2 Read the article. Answer the questions.

1 Who usually operates a lift these days?
2 Where can you still see lift operators?
3 What did lamplighters use to light the lamps?
4 How many lamps did each lamplighter light an hour?
5 What did typesetters do?
6 What did callers have to say to switchboard operators?

3 **SPEAKING** Think of two jobs that you believe will not exist when you are older. (Perhaps they are jobs you have seen in this unit.) Tell others in the class and explain why.

> *I think there won't be any cleaners when I'm older. Machines will do that job.*

WRITING

Write a short essay about your ideas from Exercise 3. Describe the jobs and explain why you believe they will not exist in the future.

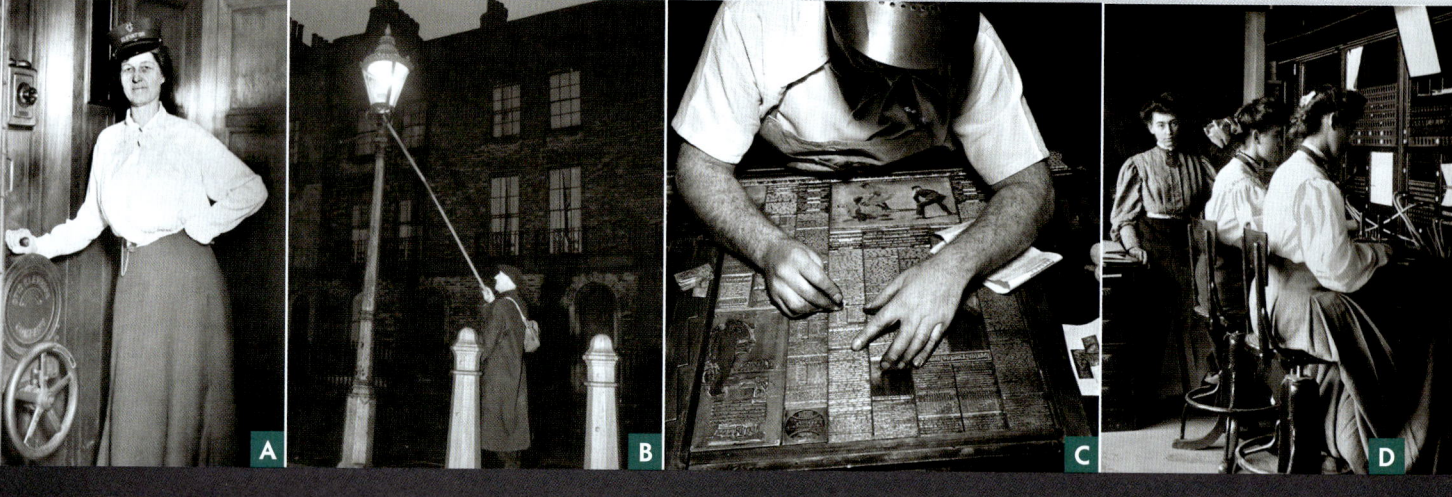

OBSOLETE JOBS

In the past, there were many jobs that now no longer exist. Most of them have been replaced by machines, but in some cases the whole idea has disappeared. For example, there used to be telegraph operators, who sent long-distance messages called telegrams. These were like an old kind of text message, but you had to ask a telegraph operator to transmit your message using a special electrical machine. So, no telegraph operators any more!

Here are some other jobs that people used to do.

Lift operators

These days we get in a lift, push the button and go. A lift can be operated by anyone, but until 1950, a lift operator travelled in the lift with passengers all the time. They were trained to operate the lifts. Lift operators have mostly gone now, though they are still used in some office buildings and tourist attractions, like the Eiffel Tower in Paris.

Lamplighters

In most big cities around the world at the beginning of the 20th century, street lamps used gas, not electricity. So, there were men who worked as lamplighters: they used to go around and light street lamps every evening with a kind of candle on a long pole. They used to light about a hundred lamps an hour. In this photo, a gas lamp is being lit by a London lamplighter.

Typesetters

A lot of computer software has been designed to help people produce books and newspapers. But how was this done before computers? The answer – the pages were assembled by typesetters. They put metal letters into wooden frames to make the layout of each page. Here, we can see newspaper pages that are being put together.

Switchboard operators

Can you believe, that in the past, to make a telephone call you had to talk to an operator, say the number you wanted and then the operator connected you to that number? Strange but true. This was one of the few jobs at the beginning of the 20th century that was almost always done by women – men were not patient enough! Here are some operators working in the USA in 1901.

Will more jobs be replaced in the next few years? It seems very possible. The world is changing so fast that new jobs are sure to appear, and others disappear.

9 WHAT A JOB!

GRAMMAR

The passive: present continuous and present perfect

1 Complete the sentences from the article on page 88 with words in the list. Then complete the rule.

has been | is being | have been | are being

1. Many jobs _____ replaced by machines.
2. Newspaper pages _____ put together.
3. A gas lamp _____ lit by a lamplighter.
4. A lot of computer software _____ designed to produce books and newspapers.

> **RULE:** The passive is formed using the verb
> 1_____ + the past participle of the main verb.
>
> - Form the present continuous passive (like sentences 2_____ and 3_____ above) using is/are being + past participle.
> - Form the present perfect passive (like sentences 4_____ and 5_____ above) using has/have been + past participle.

2 Complete the sentences with the present continuous passive or present perfect passive form of the verbs.

0. For the last 30 years, the Internet _has been used_ (use) by people all over the world.
1. New machines _____ (design) all the time.
2. Since 1950, lifts _____ (operate) by the people who get in them.
3. A lot of new medicines _____ (develop) in the last 50 years.
4. At the moment, thousands of new cars _____ (build) around the world.
5. From January 1st until now, billions of mobile phone calls _____ (make).
6. This new plane _____ (test) over 200 times.

3 Look at the pictures and make sentences about what is being done and what has been done.

The roof is being repaired.
New doors have been added.

BEFORE   NOW

➡ Workbook page 83

VOCABULARY

work as / in / for

1 Read the sentences. Then, match the verbs with the objects.

- There were men who **worked as** lamplighters.
- Marina Stuart got an offer to **work in** television.
- Harry Willsher **works for** Swizell's.

a work as   1 a company
b work for   2 an industry
c work in   3 a person in a job

2 Complete the sentences with *as*, *in* or *for*.

When my mother was young, she worked 1_____ a waitress to earn some money. After that, she was a secretary. She worked 2_____ some lawyers. Now she works 3_____ the computer industry.

My friend left school two years ago and got a job. She worked 4_____ a tour guide for about six months and really liked it. So she decided she wanted to work 5_____ the travel industry. Now she works 6_____ a travel agent in Australia.

My father works 7_____ television now. He works 8_____ a cameraman. He works 9_____ the biggest television company in the country.

> **LOOK!** *job* is a countable noun – we can use it in the plural.
> *She did four **jobs** before she became a travel agent.*
> *work* is an uncountable noun – we don't use it in the plural.
> *I have a lot of **work** to do tonight.*

work vs. job

3 Complete the sentences with *work* or *job(s)*.

0. She left school and got a ___job___.
1. Sorry, I can't talk right now, I've got a lot of _____ to do on this project.
2. When the factory closed, my uncle lost his _____ as a manager.
3. I've got a new _____ in a bank.
4. My mother is the manager of a shop. She loves her _____ because it's very interesting _____.
5. There aren't enough _____ in this town.
6. Being a street cleaner is very hard _____.
7. Sometimes I have to take _____ home at the weekend.
8. Cleaning out the garage is a big _____ for one person.

➡ Workbook page 84

PHOTOSTORY: episode 5

For a good cause

1 Look at the photos and answer the questions.
1 What are they raising money for?
2 What ideas do they have for raising money?
3 What do they decide to do in the end?

2 🔊 2.20 Now read and listen to the photostory. Check your answers.

1

RYAN Hi, Olivia. What happened to you yesterday?
OLIVIA Oh, I just didn't feel very good. I'm all right now though. By the way, here's your book back, Ryan.
RYAN Oh, thanks. Well, you missed the new headmistress's announcement yesterday.
OLIVIA Oh? What about?
LUKE We've been asked to do something for charity.
MEGAN Miss Dawes wants to raise money for the playground in the park. They really need some new things.

2

LUKE We thought the four of us could do something together. Want to join us, Olivia?
OLIVIA Well, yes, that'd be great. As long as we can have some fun, too!
RYAN That's not the point, Olivia. It's not about fun. It's about raising money for a good cause.
OLIVIA OK, OK. But what are we going to do?
MEGAN That's a good question. Ideas, anyone? What can we do to raise some money?

3

MEGAN A long walk? You know, overnight or something?
OLIVIA Hmm, could be dangerous at night.
RYAN What about a sponsored book read?
LUKE A what?
RYAN We all try to read as many books as possible in, say, two days. And people give us money for doing it.
LUKE Oh, no thanks! Surely we can think of something better than that!

4

MEGAN Look at that. Our teachers' cars are so dirty.
RYAN Ugh! You're right. They could all use a trip to the car wash, but the only one in town has been closed for a while.
LUKE That's it! A car wash!
OLIVIA Good idea. We'll set everything up right here, and people will pay us to wash their cars.
RYAN That sounds great. Megan?
MEGAN Sure. Let's tell Miss Dawes, then we can go and find buckets and sponges!

9 WHAT A JOB!

DEVELOPING SPEAKING

3 Work in pairs. Discuss what happens next in the story. Write down your ideas.

We think they wash lots of cars but no one gives them any money.

4 **EP5** Watch to find out how the story continues.

5 Choose the correct answers.

1 How much do they charge to wash one car?
   A £5   B £8   C £10

2 How does Ryan think he scratched the car?
   A There was a stone in the sponge.
   B He kicked a stone into the car.
   C His watch hit the car.

3 Why is Miss Dawes not very angry?
   A She doesn't care about the car.
   B Ryan removes the scratch completely.
   C The scratch wasn't very bad.

4 How do the four kids feel at the end?
   A They want to do it all again.
   B They're tired and happy.
   C Their backs hurt.

PHRASES FOR FLUENCY

1 Find these expressions in the story. Who says them? How do you say them in your language?

   1 By the way, …   4 Surely …
   2 … as long as …   5 … for a while.
   3 That's not the point. 6 That sounds [great].

2 Complete the conversation. Use the expressions in Exercise 1.

   A Hey. Let's have a party on Saturday. We haven't had a party ¹_____, have we?
   B ²_____ great. Where?
   A Well, I thought perhaps … my place.
   B Really? I thought your parents were really strict.
   A Yes, they are, usually.
   B ³_____ they'll be OK with a small party.
   A Well, I think so, ⁴_____ it really *is* a small party. ⁵_____ – I'm not going to invite Alison. We had a *big* argument yesterday.
   B You can tell your parents that the party won't go on late.
   A ⁶_____ My parents just don't like too a lot of noise.

WordWise
Time expressions with *in*

1 Complete the sentences from the unit so far with a phrase in the list.

   in the end | in the past | in the next few years

   1 _____, there were many jobs that now no longer exist.
   2 Will more jobs be replaced _____?
   3 What do they decide to do _____?

2 Match the questions and answers.

   1 When's your birthday?
   2 Can we go out tomorrow?
   3 When will you see your grandparents?
   4 Is it hot in your country?
   5 When's your next exam?

   a Yes, let's meet up *in* the evening.
   b It's *in* two weeks' time. I'll be fifteen.
   c *In* the summer holidays, I hope.
   d I'm not really sure but I think it's *in* June.
   e Yes, *in* the summer.

3 **SPEAKING** Work with a partner. Answer the questions in Exercise 2 so that they are true for you.

   ➡ Workbook page 84

FUNCTIONS
Accepting and refusing invitations

1 Complete the conversation.

   LUKE We thought we could do something together. _____, Olivia?
   OLIVIA Well, yes. _____.

2 Put the expressions in the list in the correct columns.

   Yes, I'd love to. | Sorry, no. But thanks for asking me.
   I'm [really] sorry, I'm afraid I can't.
   Yes, I'll [come along / join you / be there].

Accepting (Saying yes)	Refusing (Saying no)
Well, yes. That'd be great.	No, sorry, not this time.
1	3
2	4

3 **ROLE PLAY** Work in pairs. Student A: Go to page 127. Student B: Go to page 128. Role play the conversations. Invent more short dialogues to practise.

10 KEEP HEALTHY

OBJECTIVES

FUNCTIONS: talking about your health
GRAMMAR: past perfect simple; past perfect continuous; past perfect simple vs. past perfect continuous
VOCABULARY: time linkers; illness: collocations

READING

1 **SPEAKING** Look at the photos. With a partner, name the free-time activities. What others can you think of?

2 Think about the activities in Exercise 1. Answer the question and take notes.

How might the various free-time activities be good for someone's health?

3 **SPEAKING** Talk about your choices.

Cooking your own food can be good for your health. You can choose fresh ingredients, so the food is better for you.

4 🔊 2.21 Look at the statements below about someone who likes birdwatching. Read and listen to the article and decide if each statement is correct or incorrect. If it is correct, mark it A. If it's incorrect, mark it B.

1 Phoebe Snetsinger learned about her illness after she came back from Alaska.
2 When she got the bad news, she took some time to recover and then started travelling.
3 After travelling for about ten years, she had won the fight against her illness forever.
4 Only 12 other people were as successful with their bird spotting as Phoebe.
5 Phoebe liked breaking records, but she didn't care a lot about the environment.
6 When Phoebe finally died of cancer, she was on holiday doing what she loved most.
7 Just before she went on her last trip, she published her famous book *Birding on Borrowed Time*.
8 The book is both about birdwatching and the heroic way Phoebe got on with her life.

5 **SPEAKING** With a partner, correct the statements marked B.

10 KEEP HEALTHY

8,000 Birds to See Before You Die

Phoebe Snetsinger had just returned from a trip to Alaska when her doctors told her that she had cancer. She had less than a year to live. Phoebe was 50. As soon as she heard the news, she decided to spend the rest of her life doing what she loved most – watching birds.

She immediately went off to some of the world's most amazing natural paradises. Her trips were extremely hard. But Phoebe surprised her doctors and her family as she carried on travelling. A year came and went, and she was still alive. She was doing something that she loved and that helped her to be healthy for another ten years.

The cancer came back, but even then Phoebe Snetsinger decided not to stop. As she continued with her trips, the cancer went away again. By now she was becoming internationally famous in the birdwatching world. At the age of 61, when she had seen 7,530 species, she was named 'the world's leading bird spotter' by the Guinness Book of Records.

Four years later, during a trip to Mexico, she set a new record when she spotted species number 8,000: the very rare Rufous-necked Wood-Rail. Snetsinger had become a legend. Nobody had spotted so many different bird species before. In fact, at that time only 12 people around the world had seen more than 7,000 species of birds!

Phoebe's interest in birdwatching started in Minneapolis. Then she moved to Missouri with her family. There, she joined a group of people who were interested in birds, insects and plants around the Mississippi River. She became very worried about pollution and its impact on the environment. 'We have to protect nature,' she said. 'If we don't, future generations won't be able to enjoy watching these beautiful birds.'

Sadly, when Phoebe was 68, she died in a car accident on the island of Madagascar off the East African coast. She was there enjoying the hobby that had probably saved her life. She had been there for two weeks, and had added another five to her list of over 8,400 species. Four years after she died, the American Birding Association published her memoirs, *Birding on Borrowed Time*. Many people have enjoyed reading this moving book. It isn't just a story about a bird spotter's travels, but a touching human document of how her hobby helped her to live much longer than expected.

The Rufous-necked Wood Rail

THiNK VALUES

Never give up

1 Tick (✓) the sentences that show what you think you can learn from this story.

- [ ] Being passionate about things you like is extremely important.
- [ ] A hobby you really like can have a positive effect on your health.
- [ ] It's important to have friends you can trust at all times.
- [ ] You should always think positively and never give up hope!
- [ ] It's very important to eat healthy food and take enough exercise.

2 **SPEAKING** Talk to a partner. Compare which sentences you have ticked.

3 **SPEAKING** Which of the sentences you have ticked is the most important one for you? Give reasons.

GRAMMAR
Past perfect simple

1 **Read the example sentences and answer the questions. Then complete the rule.**

   *Phoebe Snetsinger **had** just **returned** from a trip to Alaska when her doctors **told** her that she had cancer.*

   1 Which of the two actions came first: her returning from a trip or what the doctors told her?

   *Four years later she **set** a new record. Nobody **had spotted** so many different bird species.*

   2 Which action came first?

   > **RULE:** When we tell a story, we often use the past perfect to talk about one event that happened before another event in the past.
   >
   > *She **died** in a car accident on Madagascar. She **had been** there for two weeks.*
   >
   > (She was there for two weeks before she died.)
   >
   > ```
   >        had been there      died
   >   |---------|---------------|-------|
   >  PAST     (two weeks)              NOW
   > ```
   >
   > Form the past perfect with *had* (or *'d*) + the _____ of the verb.

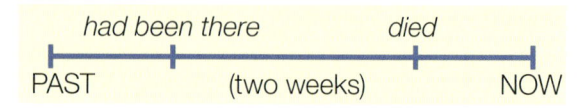

2 **Complete the sentences. Use the past perfect form of the verbs.**

   1 When I tried to phone them, nobody answered. They _____ all _____ (go) swimming.
   2 He _____ (change) so much that I almost didn't know who he was when I saw him last night.
   3 She couldn't phone me because she _____ (lose) her mobile.
   4 Somebody _____ (steal) John's car, so he was very angry.
   5 Claire had no idea I was coming to see her. Her mum _____ (forget) to tell her.
   6 You arrived too late. They _____ already _____ (leave).
   7 Her mother _____ (not give) her any money, so she couldn't buy the tickets.
   8 _____ they already _____ (return) from their holiday when you got to their house?

3 **Think about times in the past when you experienced a strong emotion. Then complete these sentences with your own words. Use the past perfect.**

   1 I was really sad because …
   2 I was absolutely delighted when I found out that …
   3 I was angry when I was told that …
   4 I was very tired after …

> Workbook page 90

VOCABULARY
Time linkers

1 **Read the story. Complete it with the words in the list.**

   when | as soon as | then | until | while

   When I was a child, I was never really very interested in nature. ¹_____ one day my aunt gave me a book for my birthday. It was called *Birding on Borrowed Time* by a woman called Phoebe Snetsinger. ²_____ she gave it me I was a little disappointed. It didn't seem very interesting, and I wanted a new game for my phone. My aunt made me promise to read it. So I did, and I loved it. It was so interesting. ³_____ I was reading the book, I completely forgot about time. In fact, I didn't do anything else ⁴_____ I'd finished it – no TV, no gaming, nothing. ⁵_____ I had finished the book, I went out and bought myself a pair of binoculars. And that's how my interest in birdwatching started.

2 **Match the parts of the sentence.**

   1 I never really liked Annie *until*
   2 *As soon as* I saw John's face
   3 *When* we got home after school
   4 *While* I was riding my bike
   5 I read the whole letter. *Then*

   a we did our homework immediately.
   b I saw it wasn't for me.
   c I realised we have a lot in common.
   d I noticed something was wrong with it.
   e I knew he was really worried.

3 **How many sentences can you make that are meaningful for you?**

   1 While I was walking to school this morning …
   2 The first thing I did when I arrived at home yesterday …
   3 I had never eaten any … until…
   4 As soon as I learnt how to (swim / play the guitar / write my name…), …
   5 I heard my favourite singer for the first time in …. Then …

> Workbook page 92

94

10 KEEP HEALTHY

LISTENING

Sam's talk:
What everybody knows: exercise is good for:
- strengthening muscles
- controlling ¹_____

4 things not everyone might know about exercise:
1. helps with mental health
   reason: there's a link between lack of ²_____ and depression.
2. strengthens your immune ³_____.
   helps you fight colds and other ⁴_____.
3. is good for your ⁵_____.
4. reduces the risk of dying from a ⁶_____ attack.

1 ►)) 2.22 Listen to 14-year-old Sam giving a talk at school. Which of these is she talking about?

1. Four things we all know about regular exercise.
2. Four things we might not know about regular exercise.
3. The advantages and disadvantages of regular exercise.

2 ►)) 2.22 Listen again. A student in Sam's class is taking notes, but she hasn't managed to write everything down. Complete her notes.

3 SPEAKING Compare your notes with a partner's. Which of the points from Sam's talk did you already know? Which were new for you?

TRAIN TO THINK

About health

1 Complete the sentences from Sam's talk with *therefore* and *you should*. Then decide in which of the sentences the speaker makes a suggestion and in which the speaker draws a conclusion?

a. Exercise gives you a healthy heart, so _____ exercise regularly. You reduce the risk of dying from a heart attack by almost a half.

b. There is a clear link between lack of movement and depression. _____ regular exercise helps you to become a happy person.

LOOK! A conclusion is only valid if it follows logically from the information given. If we need to make assumptions about facts that are not part of the information, then the conclusion is invalid.

2 SPEAKING Which of these conclusions are valid? Which are invalid? Give reasons.

A Most kinds of sports are good for your health.
Car racing is a sport.
Therefore car racing is good for your health.
valid ☐ invalid ☐

B Spending time outdoors in the fresh air is good for your health.
Birdwatching is done outdoors in the fresh air.
Therefore, birdwatching is a healthy free-time activity.
valid ☐ invalid ☐

C Vitamins are good for the immune system.
Fruit has got vitamins in it.
Therefore eating fruit is good for the immune system.
valid ☐ invalid ☐

D Positive thinking can be good for your health.
John is a positive thinker.
John will never fall ill.
valid ☐ invalid ☐

The conclusion in A is invalid. It's true that most kinds of sports are good for your health. It's also true that car racing is a sport. But it's not true that all sports are good for your health. The first sentence talks about most kinds of sports, not all sports.

READING

1 **SPEAKING** Work in pairs. Student A reads story A; student B reads story B. Tell your partner about the story you have read.

Miracle operations

A

Jack McNaughton's parents were so happy yesterday when their 4-year-old son walked through the gates of his school in Almondbank near Perth, Scotland, together with his friends.

Jack had been suffering from a serious illness since he was born and was not able to walk. A few months ago, his parents heard about a new miracle operation that doctors in a clinic in the US can perform. With help from friends and the local community, Jack's parents managed to get together the $40,000 for the operation. A team of doctors from a special clinic in Missouri operated on the young boy. After an operation of several hours the doctors said: 'We're optimistic that your son will be able to walk!' For his parents, a dream had come true. They had been waiting for this moment for years.

They are now hoping that Jack will never need to use a wheelchair again.

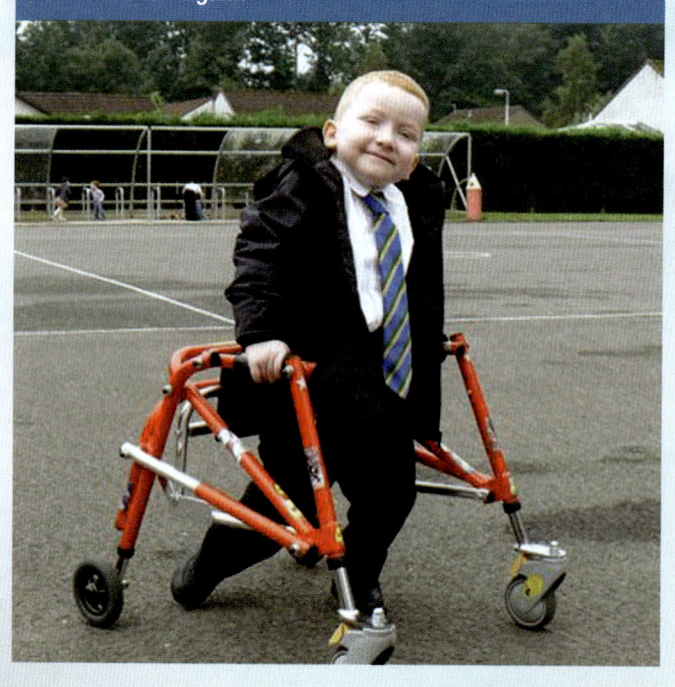

B

Doctors at the Emergency Clinic in Linz, Austria, were cautiously optimistic last night after they had operated on a boy's foot for ten hours. The boy, Jan S., had lost his foot in a skiing accident, but doctors attached the boy's foot back onto his ankle. Dr Huber and Dr Thewanger, the operating doctors, told the boy's parents there was great hope that he would be able to walk and lead a normal life again.

The 9-year-old had been taking part in a skiing race. He had been skiing on his own during the break and had not stayed with the other children. He went down a very steep slope, suddenly lost control and hit a tree. His foot was completely cut off below the ankle. Some people who had seen the accident gave first aid, and a helicopter took the boy to hospital. A few teenagers were so shocked by what they had seen that they had to get medical treatment as well.

2 Read both stories. Mark the sentences A (story A) or B (story B).

1. He had suffered for a very long time.
2. People who saw what happened were really shocked.
3. His parents had been waiting for this moment all the boy's life.
4. His parents worked hard to get the money for the operation together.
5. His parents heard that there is hope he will be able to do sport again.
6. He was doing sport and had an accident.

10 KEEP HEALTHY

GRAMMAR
Past perfect continuous

1 **Complete these examples from the stories on page 96. Circle the correct words to complete the rules.**

1 They _____ for this moment for years.
2 The 9-year-old _____ on his own during a break and had not stayed with the other children.
3 Jack _____ from a serious illness since he was born.

> **RULE:** The past perfect continuous is used for actions happening over a period of time. We can use it
> - to talk about things that started in the ¹*present / past* and continued until another time in the past.
> - to talk about things that have stopped and had a result in the ²*present / past*.
> - to focus on ³*how long / how often* an activity had been happening.

2 **Choose the correct verb for each sentence and write it in the past perfect continuous.**

walk | climb | wait | not pay | try

1 I arrived late. They _____ for 2 hours.
2 They _____ for half an hour before they realised they'd left the picnic at the hotel.
3 Our teacher got very impatient with Thomas because he _____ attention at all that day.
4 We _____ to get tickets all afternoon, but the match was sold out by noon.
5 They looked exhausted when I saw them at the top. How long _____ they _____ ?

Past perfect simple vs. past perfect continuous

3 **Complete the sentences with the past perfect simple or continuous form of the verbs.**

1 I got to my friend's house at three o'clock. They _____ already _____ football for hours. (play)
2 Before the match started, it _____ for a long time. (rain)
3 I looked at my laptop and saw that somebody _____ it. (break)
4 She _____ Spanish for years when she went to university. (study)
5 My dad got home late. He told me that there _____ an accident on the motorway. (be)

> Workbook page 91

VOCABULARY
Illness: collocations

1 **Match the sentence halves. Then underline the illness collocation in each sentence.**

0 My dad hasn't <u>taken</u> any — d
1 Our neighbour is in hospital. He had an
2 Her doctor gave her medication and she got
3 If you have a problem with your eyes, make an
4 Are you sure it's a cold? Maybe you should see
5 I ate seafood for dinner. I've been feeling

a better immediately.
b a doctor.
c appointment with a specialist soon!
d <u>exercise</u> for years now. He's not very healthy.
e sick all night.
f operation two days ago.

2 **Complete the sentences with illness collocations from Exercise 1. Use the correct forms of the verbs.**

1 I was really happy I could go to your party on Sunday. I _____ for almost a week.
2 Her knee hurts badly, and the medication she takes doesn't help. The doctors say she needs to _____ .
3 'Hello, this is Jake Miller. Can I _____ with Dr Thacker, please?'
4 I've got an earache, but I don't think it's too serious. If it's not gone in a few days I'll _____ .
5 The doctor says I'm a bit overweight and I should _____ some _____ every day.
6 Sorry to hear you're not feeling well. Hope you _____ soon.

> Workbook page 92

Pronunciation
/tʃ/ and /ʃ/ consonant sounds
Go to page 121.

FUNCTIONS
Talking about your health

SPEAKING Work in pairs. Ask and answer questions.

1 Have you ever felt sick after eating something? What happened?
2 When you have a cold, what do you do to get better?
3 Do you believe that taking exercise is good for you personally? Give reasons.
4 Where you live, is it easy or difficult to make an appointment with a doctor?
5 When you have a slight temperature, do you immediately see a doctor, or do you wait a few days?

Culture

1 Look at the pictures. Where do you think these sports events take place? Read and check your ideas.

Keeping healthy – stories from around the world

Running for fun

Running regularly helps you keep fit. That's why millions of people run several days a week and regularly take part in races. Some runners combine the sport with doing something good for others. They collect money for their run and give it to a charity. Some charity runners run a full marathon dressed in a crazy costume to collect more money for their charity.

Travis Snyder from the US had been thinking for some time about an idea for a fun run where professionals and amateurs could run together. In 2012 he organised the first 'Color Run – The happiest 5K on the planet'. What started with 6,000 participants in Phoenix, Arizona, is now held annually in many cities around the world, with millions of runners. The idea is simple: you start wearing something white, and at every kilometre people spray and paint you in different colours: 1K is yellow, 2K is blue, 3K is green, 4K is pink, ... a 'colour extravaganza!' Why do people go on a Color Run? Because 'it's healthy, fun and colourful' as one runner put it.

A beautiful morning in the park

The scene you can see in this photo is something you will see in many parks in China: big groups of people doing tai chi – slow, controlled movements of the arms and legs. These movements are very good for your health. They help to overcome stress, and people doing tai chi say it helps them to concentrate better and to feel happy and relaxed. On weekdays you will often see elderly people doing tai chi, but at weekends the parks are full of families, including children. They are all practising these elegant movements together.

Ice swimming

Imagine it's minus15 degrees Celsius outside on a sunny Saturday afternoon and you are somewhere in Russia or Finland. Would you rather see a film with a friend, go for a walk and enjoy the beautiful snow, or go for a swim in the nearby river? Not many of our readers would choose to go for a swim in such low temperatures, but in Russia, Finland and other countries, ice swimming has been popular for centuries. Some people say it's very healthy because it improves blood circulation and strengthens the body's immune system. Doctors say these things may be true, but you have to be very brave to try it – and it's only for people who are already fit and healthy!

2 ◆)) 2.25 Read and listen to the article again. Answer the questions.
1 What do ice swimmers say are the health benefits of their sport?
2 Should ice swimming be recommended to everyone? Give reasons.
3 How does a Color Run work?
4 Who came up with the idea for a Color Run and why?
5 How is tai chi good for your health?
6 Who is tai chi for?

10 KEEP HEALTHY

3 **VOCABULARY** Read the article again. Find words or phrases with the following meaning.

0 an organization that gives money, food or help to people who need it (part 1) _charity_
1 happening once every year (part 1) _____
2 to succeed in controlling a problem (part 2) _____
3 not far away (part 3) _____
4 liked by many people (part 3) _____
5 showing no fear of dangerous or difficult things (part 3) _____

4 **SPEAKING** Discuss these questions with a partner.

- Would any of the sports events in the article on page 98 attract your interest? Why (not)?
- What other fun sports events have you heard of?
- What do you do to stay fit and healthy?
- What do you think you should do more of?

WRITING
A story

1 Read Lily's story below. Answer these questions.

1 Why weren't Lily and her friends happy at lunchtime on the last day of their holiday?
2 Why do you think Pete said they couldn't go on the mountain?
3 What do you think Lily and her friends learned from the experience?

2 Which of the words in bold in the story are used to:

– talk about the time when things happened?
– talk about the order in which things happened?
– make the story more interesting?

3 Read the story again and answer the questions.

1 Which past tenses does the writer use in the first paragraph and why?
2 The story has four paragraphs. Which of them …
- sets the scene? (who? where? when?)
- explains the group's plan for that day?
- talks about a dramatic situation?
- tells about the solution to the problem?

4 Choose a sports event and think of a real or imagined story. Make a plan that helps you to tell the story in four paragraphs. Make notes about ideas for each of them.

5 Write your story (in about 200 words). Use Lily's story to help you.

- Make sure your story is well structured.
- When you have finished, check the tenses you have used.
- Find a title that you think makes people want to read your story.

A big mistake

Last summer I was staying at a holiday camp with some friends. **On the last day**, we wanted to go up a mountain near the camp. But it was **already lunchtime**, and it had been raining **all morning**. So Pete, our guide, said, 'Sorry, guys, the weather is just too bad. We can't go.' We had all been looking forward to this mountain trip for days.

At first, we were really disappointed. **Then** one of my friends had an idea. 'Why don't we go anyway?' he said. 'Pete won't notice, and we'll be back before it gets dark'. **Five minutes later** we were ready to leave.

We made good progress. 'We'll be at the top of the mountain in an hour,' we thought. But then the weather changed. It became foggy, and the rain became much stronger. **Suddenly**, we realised that we had lost our way.

Luckily, I had my mobile phone on me. We phoned Pete at the camp. He told us to stay where we were. When he found us, it was already dark. We were really sorry. We had made a big mistake.

CAMBRIDGE ENGLISH: Preliminary

THiNK EXAMS

READING
Part 4: Four-option multiple choice

Workbook page 97

1 Read the text and questions below. For each question, mark the correct letter A, B, C or D.

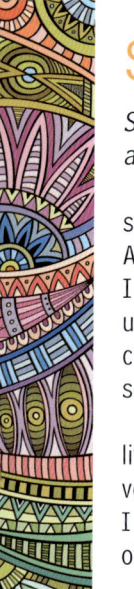

Somewhere in Africa

Seventeen-year-old Nadia Clarke talks about her African experience.

Last summer I got the chance to spend a month helping out in a hospital in Africa. I had one year left at school, and I was interested in studying medicine at university. I thought it was the perfect chance to get some experience and to see if I really wanted to be a doctor.

It was a month that changed my life. I was introduced to a world that is very different to mine in so many ways. I was horrified at how poor so many of the families over there are and how difficult their lives can be. But I was also amazed at how positively people go about their everyday lives. The way they come together and help each other is a real inspiration, and something I think a lot of us here in the UK have forgotten. I think many of us don't realise how lucky we are.

My work in the hospital was hard. I spent a lot of time cleaning floors and changing bed sheets, but I also got to spend some time looking after the patients. And I got the chance to talk to some doctors and ask them about the profession. I saw some truly awful things in the hospital, but none of them changed my mind about being a doctor. In fact, they only made me more determined to do medicine!

When I finish, I know exactly what I'm going to do: I want to work for an international organisation like the Red Cross or Médecins sans Frontières and spend my life helping people overseas who haven't been as lucky in life as me. I can't wait to get started.

1 What is Nadia doing in the text?
  A Describing how to get work in a hospital.
  B Comparing hospitals in the UK and Africa.
  C Giving advice to people who want to be doctors.
  D Talking about an amazing experience she had.

2 What did Nadia notice most about people there?
  A How little money all of them had.
  B How friendly the people were to her.
  C How well they looked after each other.
  D How much they needed medical help.

3 How has the trip changed Nadia's ideas about her own future?
  A She doesn't want to be a doctor any more.
  B Now she definitely wants to be a doctor in the UK.
  C It's made her change a lot of her opinions.
  D Now she really knows what she wants to do with her life.

4 What might Nadia write home to her parents?
  A The doctors have been really kind here, but I'm not so sure it's what I want to do anymore.
  B The people are very friendly and I've made some really good friends.
  C It's been difficult, but I really want to work somewhere like this when I'm a doctor.
  D Sweeping floors and cleaning beds! I want to spend more time with the patients.

LISTENING
Part 3: Gap fill

Workbook page 53

2 ◼)) 2.26 You will hear a man talking about summer jobs at the local newspaper. For each question, fill in the missing information in the numbered space.

The Daily Post

SUMMER HOLIDAY JUNIOR POSITIONS
- Two journalists
- Two [1] _____
- One editor

Working week
- Mondays and [2] _____ – 1 pm to 6 pm
- Tuesdays and Thursdays – 8 am – 1 pm
- [3] _____ free!
- £5 an hour

Other info
Job is for four weeks starting on Monday [4] _____ .

Application forms on website or in [5] _____ – this week only!

Phone Robin on [6] _____ for more information.

100

TEST YOURSELF

UNITS 9 & 10

VOCABULARY

1 Complete the sentences with the words in the list. There are two extra words.

as soon as | until | then | as | career | notice | challenging | take | feel | in | make | training

1. If you aren't sleeping very well, perhaps you should _____ more exercise.
2. My brother's working _____ a secretary for the summer.
3. Have you ever thought about a _____ in marketing?
4. The job's OK, but it isn't very _____, so sometimes I don't enjoy it much.
5. At the beginning, we got lots of on-the-job _____ so we could do it properly.
6. My mum used to be a teacher, but now she works _____ the travel industry.
7. She hated the job, so after a month, she gave in her _____.
8. I'm going to keep trying _____ I find the answer!
9. I don't feel well. I'm going to phone the doctor and _____ an appointment.
10. I'll call you _____ I get home.

/10

GRAMMAR

2 Complete the sentences. Use the correct form of the verbs in the list.

build (x2) | invite (x2) | work (x2)

1. After I left school, I _____ in a shop.
2. Our school _____ in 1965.
3. We _____ to a party next Saturday, but I don't know if we can go.
4. My mum _____ in the bank for 20 years when she left her job there.
5. Every year, my sister _____ to talk at a conference, and she always says 'Yes.'
6. They _____ their house in only six months!

3 Find and correct the mistake in each sentence.

1. Millions of hamburgers eat every day.
2. When we got to London, we had being travelling for a long time.
3. Hundreds of houses have damaged by the hurricane.
4. The baby was very ill, so they were taken her to hospital.
5. Last week, I hurt in a car accident.
6. When she left school, she was a student there for eight years.

/12

FUNCTIONAL LANGUAGE

4 Write the missing words. Choose from the words in the list.

about | afraid | better | feeling | hurts | see | together | would

1. A My leg _____ really badly.
   B Oh, really? Perhaps you should go and _____ a doctor.
2. A Joanna, how _____ coming to the cinema tonight?
   B Well, yes, that _____ be great. Thanks.
3. A I haven't been _____ well all week.
   B Oh, I'm sorry to hear that. Hope you get _____ soon.
4. A I thought we could do something _____ tomorrow.
   B I'm really sorry, but I'm _____ I can't.

/8

MY SCORE /30

22 – 30
10 – 21
0 – 9

101

11 MAKING THE NEWS

OBJECTIVES

FUNCTIONS: reporting what someone has said; expressing feelings: anger
GRAMMAR: reported statements; verb patterns: object + infinitive
VOCABULARY: fun; more verbs with object + infinitive; expressions with *make*

READING

1 Tick (✓) the qualities you need to be a news journalist.

- [ ] funny
- [ ] intelligent
- [ ] brave
- [ ] confident
- [ ] charming
- [ ] talented
- [ ] positive
- [ ] active
- [ ] cheerful
- [ ] warm
- [ ] serious
- [ ] adventurous

2 **SPEAKING** Work in pairs. What other adjectives can you think of?

3 **SPEAKING** Would you like to be a journalist? Say why or why not.

> I'd like to be a journalist because I like finding out things.

> I wouldn't like to be a journalist because I'm not adventurous.

4 On April Fool's Day in many English-speaking countries, people play jokes on others. Journalists are usually serious, but sometimes they play jokes, too. Do you have a similar day in your country?

5 🔊 2.27 Read and listen to the article. Which photo relates to each story? Write the dates of the stories on the pictures to match them.

6 Read the article again. Which story are these people talking about?

1 'I saw that. I think they were in the middle of making a nature programme.'
2 'What a great way to get people interested in your product.'
3 'They said the mistake happened because of a bad translation.'
4 'It definitely doesn't come from a plant. I think it's made with flour and water.'
5 'I think people believed the story because he was such an intelligent person.'

April Fool's Day

In **1957** the BBC news programme Panorama told its viewers that Swiss farmers were enjoying a really good year for their spaghetti crop. They showed a film of the farmers picking the pasta from their trees. Many people believed the story and some of them even phoned up the BBC to ask how they could grow their own spaghetti tree. The date, of course, was April 1st, or April Fool's Day – the day when people in many countries across the world like to play jokes on each other.

April 1st seems to be very popular with journalists. They have the extremely important job of reporting the news to us. For 364 days a year they need to be serious. But for one day a year they allow themselves to forget this responsibility for a few minutes and have a bit of fun trying to fool their readers or viewers.

11 MAKING THE NEWS

There are many great examples of funny April Fool's Day jokes from the newspapers and TV.

For example, in **2008** BBC News claimed that penguins could fly. It said that their cameraman had seen this happen while filming at the South Pole. He said that, luckily, he had filmed the event, and they showed some video of penguins taking off and flying through the air. Of course, the BBC later admitted they had made up the whole story and used special effects to create the film.

In **1981** the Daily Mail had a story about a Japanese runner in the London marathon. The man was still running days after the race had finished. The story explained that the athlete had misunderstood the rules of the race. Instead of running for 26 miles, he believed he needed to run for 26 days. The paper said that he was lost somewhere in the middle of the British countryside.

And there's certainly nothing new about these types of stories. Back in **1878** The Daily Graphic newspaper in the USA had a story about the famous scientist Thomas Edison. It told its readers that Edison had invented a food machine that would feed the human race. It didn't explain how the machine worked, just that it would make any kind of food using air, water and earth. Many people believed the story and Edison got letters from people all over the country.

It's not just journalists who enjoy trying to fool us. Many big companies have joined in the fun over the years. In **1998** a famous fast food restaurant used a whole page advert in one of the daily newspapers to tell us that it was going to sell a hamburger for left-handed people. It said that the new burger was just the same as the normal burger, but they had turned all the ingredients 180° in the bun. They said it would be easier for left-handed people to eat. Thousands of people went to restaurants to try and buy one.

So when people tell you not to believe everything you read in the newspapers, they might be right – especially on April 1st!

THINK VALUES

Being able to laugh at yourself

1 **SPEAKING** Three people were told about the spaghetti trees. They all believed the story. Here's what they said when they found out the truth. In pairs, discuss each reaction. Whose reaction do you like most? Why?

   1 'How could I believe that? I feel really stupid and embarrassed.'
   2 'It's a really great story. I think it's funny that I believed it.'
   3 'It is funny, but I do feel a bit silly for believing it.'

   Number 1 is too serious. It was just a silly joke. It's not important ...

2 **SPEAKING** Work in pairs. Think of a time when you were the target of a joke. How did you feel? Do you feel differently about it now?

   I remember once my friend ...
   At the time I felt / I didn't think ...
   Now I ...

3 **SPEAKING** Discuss in pairs.
   1 Think of a time when a joke went wrong. What was it and why did it go wrong?
   2 Why do you need to be careful when thinking about playing a joke?

GRAMMAR
Reported statements

1 **Look at the article on pages 102–03 again. How are these statements reported? Write down how the underlined words change. Then use the example sentences to complete the rules.**

0 Swiss farmers <u>are enjoying</u> a really good year for their spaghetti crop. *were enjoying*
1 Penguins <u>can</u> fly. _____
2 Our cameraman <u>saw</u> this happen at the South Pole. _____
3 He <u>is</u> lost somewhere in the middle of the British countryside. _____
4 Edison <u>has invented</u> a food machine that will feed the human race. _____
5 The restaurant <u>is going to</u> sell a hamburger for left-handed people. _____
6 It <u>will</u> be easier for left-handed people to eat. _____

> **RULE:** When we report what people say, we often change the verb tenses:
> - present simple → *past simple*
> - present continuous → _____
> - past simple → _____
> - present perfect → _____
> - am/is/are going to → _____
> - can/can't → _____
> - will/won't → _____
>
> We often use the verbs *say* and *tell* to report.
> After *tell*, use an object (*me, her, them*, etc.). After *say*, don't use an object.

2 **Complete the sentences with *say* or *tell*.**

0 My dad *told* me that he wanted me to tidy my room.
1 The teacher _____ us that we could go home early.
2 I _____ that I was going to phone you when I got home.
3 The weatherman _____ that it would be sunny later.
4 She _____ him that she hadn't forgotten his birthday.
5 They _____ that they were visiting their grandparents on Saturday.
6 He _____ that he had left the books at the front desk for me.
7 Dad _____ us we could stay at the party until eleven.
8 He _____ that someone was following him, but I _____ him he was imagining it.

3 **Rewrite these quotes as reported speech.**

0 'I work really hard.' (He said …)
   He said that he worked really hard.
1 'I flew back from Africa on Friday.' (She told …)
2 'We've met lots of interesting people.' (They said …)
3 'I'm going to write a book one day.' (He told …)
4 'I can work for two days without sleeping.' (You said …)
5 'We'll call you from the airport.' (They told …)
6 'I'm working on a really interesting story.' (She said …)
7 'I need a holiday.' (He told …)
8 'I wanted to see the movie on opening night.' (She told …)

> Workbook page 100

VOCABULARY
Fun

1 **Work in pairs. Cover sentences a–h. Read sentences 1–8 and think of a sentence to follow each one to explain the meaning of the word in italics.**

1 The party was *fun*.
2 I love Steve. He's *hilarious*.
3 Why is everyone *laughing* at me?
4 I don't *get* that *joke*.
5 We *played* a *joke* on him.
6 I'm rubbish at *telling jokes*.
7 I'm not sure she liked you *making fun* of her.
8 That's not *funny* at all.

a Did I say something silly?
b I always forget the endings.
c She seems quite upset.
d We had a really great time.
e Please don't do it again.
f I mean he's really, really funny.
g But I'm not sure he thought it was funny.
h Can someone explain it to me?

2 **Match sentences 1–8 with the sentences a–h.**

3 **SPEAKING Discuss in pairs.**

1 Who's the funniest person you know?
2 Are you good at telling jokes? Why or why not?
3 Do you always get jokes? What do you do when you don't understand?
4 Have you ever played a good joke on someone? What was it?
5 What's the funniest thing you have ever done?

> Workbook page 102

11 MAKING THE NEWS

WRITING
A news report

Choose one of the headlines below and write a short news report for it. Try to include two examples of reported speech.

> **Found – the world's funniest joke**
> # GOOD JOKE GOES WRONG
> **Fun for everyone at school party**

LISTENING

1 Which of these words do you associate with the extreme weather conditions in the photos?

snow | wind | ice | rain

1. tornado
2. blizzard 
3. flood 
4. hailstorm 

2 🔊 2.28 Warren Faidley is an extreme weather journalist. Listen and tick (✓) the types of weather in Exercise 1 that he reports on. Then answer the question.

What is the difference between a weatherman and a weather journalist?

3 🔊 2.28 Listen again. Choose the correct picture and put a tick (✓) in the box below it.

1 How did he escape from the river when he was 12?
   A  B  C 

2 What danger did he escape from with his father when he was a child?
   A  B  C 

3 Which of these photos gave Faidley his lucky break?
   A  B  C 

4 Which of these is the charity that Faidley has started? 
   A STORM AID B STORM SURVIVORS SOCIETY C STORM ANGEL CHASE THEM

THiNK SELF-ESTEEM

Giving an award

1 You want to create an international prize called the Warren Faidley Award. Who will this prize be given to?

☐ A very brave journalist   ☐ A great photographer   ☐ A weather scientist

2 Think of people you admire and create an award in their name. They can be famous people or people you know. Who should receive the award?

> The Miss Allen Award is for the best teacher.

> The Michelle Obama Award is for someone who has done something special for women.

105

READING

1. Imagine you are going to be interviewed by a journalist on a TV programme for teenagers about a subject you know a lot about. Think about the questions and make notes.

    1 What is your specialist subject?
    Arsenal
    2 What do you know about it?
    all the players, the history of the club

2. **SPEAKING** Work in pairs. Tell your partner about your specialist subject and what you can say about it.

    > My specialist subject is Arsenal. I can tell you about all the players. I can tell you where they are from, how old they are ...

3. Read the article. Match the people with the descriptions.

    1 Guy Goma   a an expert
    2 Guy Kewney   b a candidate for a job
    3 Karen Bowerman   c a journalist

4. Read the article again. Put the events in the order they happened. Write 1–8 in the boxes.

    ☐ Mr Goma gives his opinion about downloading music.
    ☐ Mr Goma is taken to a reception area.
    ☐ The TV presenter suspects she's got the wrong man.
    ☐ Mr Goma is asked his first name.
    ☐ Mr Goma is taken to a studio.
    ☐ Mr Goma has his job interview.
    ☐ Mr Goma arrives at the BBC television centre.
    ☐ Mr Goma says he is surprised about the court case.

A tale of two Guys

When Guy Goma went for a job interview at the BBC he was very surprised by the questions the interviewer was asking him. He'd applied for a job in the computing department. Why did the woman want him to answer questions about a big legal case involving a famous music company? He was even more surprised when he found that he was answering these questions live on television.

Mr Goma had been waiting in a reception room at Television Centre when an assistant came up and asked him if he was Guy. When he said 'yes', she told him to follow her to a TV studio. The next thing he knew, he was on national television. At the same time, Guy Kewney, the editor of Newswireless.net, sat in another reception room wondering why he was waiting so long.

Mr Goma later described the interview as being 'very stressful' but he did his best to answer the questions from the BBC business journalist Karen Bowerman. At first, Mr Goma looked very nervous, but after a while he seemed to be enjoying himself. When Karen asked him to talk about the result of the court case, he said that it was 'a big surprise'. He then went on to say that more and more people were downloading music from the Internet because it was very easy. At that point Karen Bowerman appeared to realise something was wrong and very professionally ended the interview after only three questions.

Afterwards, Mr Goma said his interview had been very short but that he'd be happy to come back any time in the future to talk on national television. However, he asked to be given a few more minutes to 'get ready' next time.

Guy Goma at BBC Television Centre

The video of Mr Goma was quickly uploaded onto YouTube, where it immediately went viral.

Twenty minutes after his TV appearance, Mr Goma finally got to his real interview. Unfortunately, he did not get the job.

11 MAKING THE NEWS

GRAMMAR
Verb patterns: object + infinitive

1 **Put the words in order to make sentences from the text. Then complete the rule.**

1 her / him / She / to / told / follow
   _____

2 the court case / Karen / him / to talk about / asked / the result of
   _____

3 questions / wanted / woman / answer / him / to / The
   _____

> **RULE:** Some verbs (*ask*, *want*, *tell*) are followed by an object (noun or personal ¹_____) and the ²_____ form of the verb.
> *Mum **asked me to tidy** my room.*

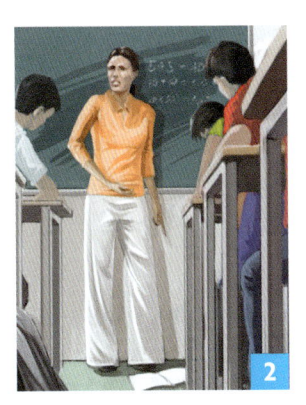

2 **Look at pictures 1–4. What does the teacher ask the students to do? Write sentences.**

1 *Can you put the books over there please?*
2 _____
3 _____
4 _____

3 **Work in pairs. Take turns to report the sentences in Exercise 2. Use *tell* and *ask*.**

> *She asked him to carry her books.*

→ Workbook page 101

VOCABULARY
More verbs with object + infinitive

1 **Read what the people say. Match each one with a verb from the list.**

persuade | encourage | warn | invite
remind | allow | want

0 'We think you'll arrive by eight o'clock.' _expect_
1 'Slow down. You're going to crash.' _____
2 'Don't forget to watch the programme.' _____
3 'OK, you can go to the party.' _____
4 'You should definitely enter the talent show. You're a really good singer.' _____
5 'Take me to the One Direction concert – please. I'll be really good. I promise. You will? Oh, thank you!' _____
6 'I've chosen you to play in the school tennis team.' _____
7 'Would you like to go to the cinema?' _____

2 **Rewrite the sentences in Exercise 1 with the verbs you matched to each one.**

> *They expected me to arrive by eight o'clock.*

→ Workbook page 102

SPEAKING

1 **Think about these things. Make notes about them.**

1 Two things your parents allow you to do.
2 Two things your parents expect you to do.
3 Two things your parents warn you not to do.

2 **Work in pairs. Talk about your thoughts from Exercise 1.**

> *My parents allow me to watch TV until 9 pm.*

3 **Now discuss these things with your partner.**

1 Two things you expect your parents to do for you.
2 Two things you don't expect your parents to do for you any more.
3 Two things you expect your parents to do your whole life – even if you don't want them to.

Pronunciation
Intonation: rude or polite?
Go to page 121.

PHOTOSTORY: episode 6

The journalist

1 Look at the photos and answer the questions.
   Why is Megan cross?
   What are the two newspaper stories about?

2 🔊 2.31 Now read and listen to the photostory. Check your answers.

1

LUKE What's up, Megan? You don't look too happy.
MEGAN I'm not. Check this out. 'Teenagers in graffiti disgrace – Local teenagers vandalise town centre once again.'
OLIVIA What!? Let me see.
MEGAN Do you see that? 'Once again'!! Like it happens every day!

2

OLIVIA It makes me so angry when I read headlines like this.
LUKE Don't get too angry, guys. It's not worth it.
RYAN Sorry, Luke, I don't agree. We're talking about this journalist, what's his name, Nigel Forsyth, who doesn't like teenagers.
OLIVIA That's right. My dad heard him on the radio once, and he was like: Oh, teenagers, all they do is make trouble.
LUKE I'm just saying that we can't really do anything about it, that's all.
MEGAN Hmm!

3

A WEEK LATER
MEGAN You're not going to believe this.
RYAN What now?
MEGAN Nigel Forsyth's latest story: 'Wild teenagers out of control – Park buildings ruined by spray paint.' Someone sprays a little paint on one old wall, and this is how he tells the story.
OLIVIA Yeah, and it was probably just one person, but he's talking about 'wild teenagers', plural. I don't believe it.

4

MEGAN One person does something stupid and we're all criminals.
RYAN I know what you mean. It's just, well, infuriating.
MEGAN Nigel Forsyth! Hah! Well, that's enough! I'm going to have a word with him. I'm going to make sure that he knows one thing: the young people of this town are not wild criminals!

11 MAKING THE NEWS

DEVELOPING SPEAKING

3 Work in pairs. Discuss what happens next in the story. Write down your ideas.

We think Megan is going to write to the paper and complain.

4 ▶ EP6 Watch to find out how the story continues.

5 Decide if the statements are correct (✓) or incorrect (✗).

1. Megan wants to turn the bad things into good things.
2. Ryan asks Megan why she never tells them anything.
3. Mr Lane gives them permission to go ahead with the project.
4. Megan speaks in a school assembly.
5. Not many kids help.
6. Megan is happy with the story about their work.
7. Nigel Forsyth is now Megan's friend.

PHRASES FOR FLUENCY

1 Find these expressions in the story. Who says them? How do you say them in your language?

1. Check [this] out. _____
2. It's not worth it. _____
3. We're talking about … _____
4. He was like …[direct speech] _____
5. I'm just saying … _____
6. have a word [with someone] _____

2 Use the expressions in Exercise 1 above to complete the dialogues.

1. A Why don't you ask James to help you?
   B James? ¹_____ a guy who just does whatever he wants!
   A Yes, but you never know.
   B ²_____. He never listens to anything I say.
2. A Did you talk to Alex about the match?
   B Yes. But ³_____ : 'No way, you can't play and that's that.'
   A Really? That's bad. Should I ⁴_____ him?
   B No, it's OK, thanks.
3. A Hey, ⁵_____. It's a new mobile phone, and it's brilliant.
   B I really don't care.
   A Well, you don't need to be rude.
   B Oh, I'm sorry. ⁶_____ that I'm not interested in phones.

WordWise
Expressions with *make*

1 Complete the expressions from the unit so far with a word from the list.

fun | friends | angry | up | sure | difference

1. The BBC **made** _____ the story about the flying penguins.
2. She didn't like you **making** _____ of her.
3. It **makes** me so _____.
4. I'm going to **make** _____ that he knows that most young people are not criminals.
5. Together we can **make** a _____.
6. Megan **made** _____ with Nigel Forsyth.

2 Complete the sentences with *make* + another word.

1. When you go out, _____ that the door's locked, OK?
2. Doing a lot of exercise can _____ a _____ to your health.
3. When you move to a new school, it can be difficult to _____ with people.
4. It isn't very nice to _____ of other people.
5. Is that story really true? Or did you _____ it _____?
6. Those newspaper stories are not accurate. They really _____ me _____.

➡ Workbook page 102

FUNCTIONS
Expressing feelings: anger

1 Complete the expressions with the words in the box.

cross | makes | hate | so

1. I get _____ angry
2. It _____ me really angry   when …
3. I _____ it
4. It makes me really _____

2 Make a list of the top three things that make you angry. Write sentences using the phrases above.

I get so angry when my brother takes my things.

3 SPEAKING Work in pairs. Tell each other about the things on your lists.

12 PLAYING BY THE RULES

OBJECTIVES

FUNCTIONS: talking about permission; following and giving simple instructions
GRAMMAR: *be allowed to / let*; third conditional
VOCABULARY: discipline; consequences and reasons

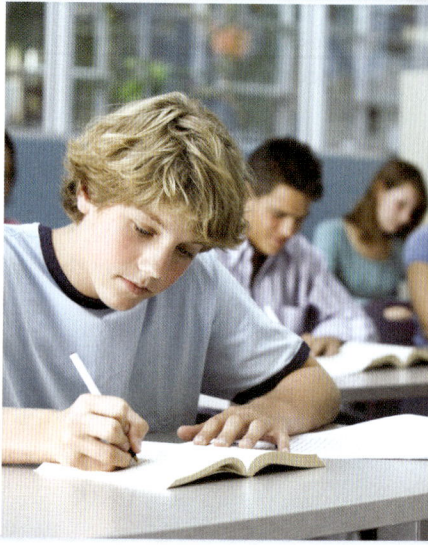

READING

1 Look at this list. Put a tick (✓) if it's something you can do. Put a cross (✗) if it's something you can't do.

- [ ] stay up late at weekends
- [ ] invite friends to your house
- [ ] watch any TV programme you want
- [ ] wear any clothes you want at home
- [ ] wear any clothes you want to school
- [ ] use your mobile phone at school
- [ ] listen to music in your bedroom
- [ ] hang out with your friends in town

2 What other things can you think of that you can or can't do at home or at school?

3 **SPEAKING** Work with a partner. Who has stricter rules in their life?

4 Look at the pictures with the article on the next page. In what way did these children have a hard life?

5 ⏵ 2.32 Read and listen to the article. Under each picture write *Greek*, *Aztec* or *both*.

6 Read the article again and complete the sentences. Use between one and three words.

1 Ancient Greek parents had _____ to decide if they wanted to keep their babies.
2 Unwanted babies often became _____ .
3 Unlike Greek girls, Greek boys _____ .
4 At military school Greek boys didn't often have _____ to eat.
5 _____ awaited Aztec children who broke the rules.
6 Ancient Aztecs thought education _____ .
7 Aztec boys and girls _____ to the same school.
8 *Calmecac* schools were for children from _____ .

THINK VALUES

The importance of rules

1 Read the statements a–d. Which one is:
   1 a personal rule? ☐   3 a school rule? ☐
   2 a family rule? ☐   4 a rule of society? ☐

   a You're not allowed to ride bikes on the pavements.
   b Our parents don't let us leave the dinner table before everyone has finished.
   c I make sure that I tidy my room every weekend.
   d You can't ask a question unless you put your hand up.

2 **SPEAKING** Work in pairs. Think of more rules (at least one each) for the four areas: *personal*, *family*, *school*, *society*. What is the punishment for breaking your rules?

Hard times to be a kid

'I'm not allowed to stay out late.'

'Why do I have to do my homework before I can watch TV?'

'My parents never let me go to parties.'

'Why is it just Mum and Dad who make the rules? Life's just not fair.'

Do these complaints sound familiar? Well, if you think your life is hard, you might like to think about kids in ancient times. For some of them, life was really hard.

If you were born in ancient Greece, you weren't even thought to be a real person until you'd been alive for five days. That's right – for five days after you were born, your parents were allowed to get rid of you. If they decided they didn't want you, they'd just leave you outside somewhere to die. Of course, you might get lucky and someone else might pick you up, but then you'd spend the rest of your life as their slave. However, if your parents decided that they wanted you as part of the family, then there was a special ceremony to welcome you.

Only the boys were allowed to go to school. Greek girls stayed at home, where their mothers taught them skills like cooking and weaving – things that would help them find a husband.

At the age of seven, some boys were sent away to very strict military schools, where they were taught how to become soldiers. Life was pretty hard at these schools. For example, the kids were often hungry. The teachers didn't let them have much food – for a reason. They wanted the boys to learn how to survive for themselves by stealing food. But if they got caught, they were punished.

Aztec children in Central America also had a difficult life in ancient times. If they broke rules, they could expect some pretty nasty punishments.

On the good side, Aztecs really believed in the importance of schooling. In the home, children learned practical skills: dads taught their sons how to fish and farm while mothers taught their daughters home-making skills. Girls and boys also went to school (although the adults didn't let them go to the same schools).

Kids went to schools called *telpochcalli*. They had lessons about history, religion and music. The boys also had lessons in how to fight. If the children were from a more important family, they went to a *calmecac* where they learned how to read and write, too.

At both schools children had to be on their best behaviour. They knew all about the punishments for behaving badly, and life was hard enough anyway.

GRAMMAR
be allowed to / let

1 Look at the example sentences. Then complete the rules with *be allowed to* and *let*.

1. I'm not allowed to stay out late.
2. My parents never let me go to parties.
3. For five days after you were born, your parents were allowed to get rid of you.
4. The teachers didn't let them have much food.

> **RULE:** To talk about permission we can use *be allowed to* and *let*.
>
> We use ¹_____ when there's no need to identify who gives (or doesn't give) the permission. The subject of the sentence is the person who receives (or doesn't receive) the permission.
> - Form this with subject + ²_____ (not) + allowed to + ³_____ . It is a passive construction.
>
> We use ⁴_____ when the subject of the sentence is (or isn't) giving the permission.
> - Form this with subject + ⁵_____ + [person] + verb.

2 Rewrite the sentence using the words in brackets.

0. My parents don't let me go out on school nights. (I / allowed)
   I'm not allowed to go out on school nights.
1. I wasn't allowed to go to the party. (My parents / let)
2. My mum didn't let me walk to school on my own until I was 12. (I / allowed)
3. We aren't allowed to text in class. (The teacher / let)
4. My dad lets me play his electric guitar. (I / allowed)
5. My sister is allowed to stay up until 11 pm on Saturday nights. (Dad / let)

3 Choose three of the activities in the list and write two true and one false sentence about yourself.
- listen to loud music in my bedroom
- watch TV before school
- use my mobile during dinner
- go to the cinema by myself
- buy my own clothes
- meet my friends on a school night

4 **SPEAKING** Work in pairs. Read out your sentences. Can your partner guess which sentence isn't true?

> *My parents let me go out on a school night.* — *That isn't true.*

Workbook page 108

VOCABULARY
Discipline

1 Match the phrases 1–6 with the definitions a–f.
1. to do what you're told
2. to behave well
3. to get punished
4. to break the rules
5. to get into trouble
6. to get told off

a. to be good by acting in the correct way
b. to do something you shouldn't do
c. to have problems because you did something wrong
d. to follow the rules that others make
e. to be told that what you did was wrong
f. to be made to do something you don't want to do because you did something wrong

2 Complete the sentences with phrases from Exercise 1, above. Sometimes there is more than one possible answer.

1. My sister Claire breaks all the school rules, so she always gets _____ .
2. Kenny always _____ in class. The teacher thinks he's perfect.
3. His Mum and Dad would be a lot happier if sometimes he _____ .
4. My little brother Stan is really naughty. He's always getting _____ .
5. Julia's a rebel. She likes _____ .
6. If I don't behave well, I usually get _____ .

3 Which of the children in Exercise 2 do you think these pictures show?

4 **SPEAKING** Which sentences are true for you? Compare with your partner.
- I always do what I'm told.
- I often get told off by my parents and teachers.
- I'm always getting into trouble.
- I never break the rules. I think rules are important!
- I think people should get punished for bad behaviour.
- If you behave well all the time, it's boring!

Workbook page 110

12 PLAYING BY THE RULES

LISTENING

1 ◁)) 2.33 Listen to Sam talking about a game called *rock, paper, scissors*. Which object or animal does each of these hand positions show?

The modern game   *The ancient game of* mushi-ken

1 _____   4 _____

2 _____   5 _____

3 _____   6 _____

2 ◁)) 2.33 Listen again and answer the questions.
1 Which object beats the rock in the modern game and why?
2 Which object is beaten by the rock in the modern game and why?
3 How old is the earliest version of this game?
4 Where was Mushi-ken played?
5 How do the animals defeat each other in Mushi-ken?
6 How often do the world championships of the modern game take place?

FUNCTIONS
Following and giving simple instructions

1 Think of a simple game you like to play that needs two or more people. Answer the questions and make notes.
- What do you need to play? Dice? Cards?

- How many players are needed to play the game?
- How do the players know when it is their turn to play?
- Do the players score points? If yes, how?
- What are the players *not* allowed to do?

2 **SPEAKING** Work in pairs. Describe to each other how to play the game.

Before you start, …   Then, …
So how do you play?   Finally, …
First, …   The first player to …

TRAIN TO THiNK

Play *rock, paper, scissors*

1 What do you think these hand positions could represent?

I think number one could be water.

1    2    3

2 Follow the instructions and make a new version of *rock, paper, scissors*.
1 Think of three things to do battle, e.g. water, fire and air.
2 Think about how the objects defeat each other.
- Water defeats fire because it puts it out.
- Fire defeats air because it consumes it.
- Air defeats water because it dries it.
3 Think of a hand position for each of the things.
4 Explain your game to your partner and play it.

READING

1 Read the results of a contest carried out by a fiction writing website. Match the pictures with the stories.

www.FabFiction.co.uk/7fy8d73m

Small is beautiful. So every week we invite our readers to send us their (very) short stories. Each story must be exactly 50 words, not a word more, not a word less – just like this introduction. (Words like 'didn't' count as one word.) And then we publish all our favourites!

Here are the best from last week's theme: Breaking the Rules

1 The sign clearly said 'Don't feed the seagulls'. Maybe if the seagull had been able to read, it wouldn't have flown down and stolen my sandwich. Unfortunately, it couldn't read. It flew down and it stole my lunch. And that's why I'm still hungry. Can I have a cheese sandwich, please? Please?

2 'If we had run, we wouldn't have missed the train,' she said angrily.
'I don't like following your orders,' he replied, as the 10 pm train was leaving the station. 'We'll get the next train.'
'That's no problem,' said the guard standing nearby. 'It leaves at eight o'clock tomorrow morning. Good night.'

3 'Never, ever go into the abandoned old house at the end of the road.' That's what all the parents told their children. One day Jack decided to find out what the mystery was all about and went into the house. Now there's a new mystery in town: what exactly happened to Jack?

4 The big sign at the park gates said: 'No ball games. No cycling. No skateboarding. No picnics.' We stood and looked at it for a long time. 'Let's go in anyway,' I said. My friend replied: 'No way! No fun!' I smiled. 'No problem!' I said, and then took down the sign.

5 If I hadn't listened to my mother, I wouldn't have got into trouble. 'Always tell the truth,' she said. So when Miss Green asked me why I was yawning, I told her the truth – I thought the lesson was really, really boring. Now I've got to explain all this to the headmaster.

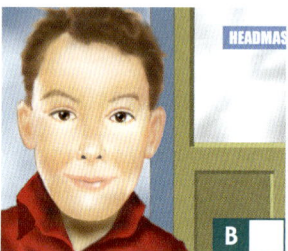

A   B   C   D   E

2 Match the stories (1–5) to the titles. Write the numbers. There is one title you won't need.
   a Where can we play?
   b A long wait
   c A question with no answer
   d A game with no rules
   e Birds don't read
   f Trouble at school

3 Each of the stories actually has 52 words. Find two words that you can take out in each one. (There are always more than two possibilities!)

4 Which of the stories are these people talking about? Do you agree with them?
   a 'Sometimes it's a good idea not to tell the truth.'
   b 'I would never go into a place like that.'
   c 'It's his own fault that he had to wait.'
   d 'We need to find a way to keep birds away from people.'
   e 'It's crazy for public places to have so many rules.'

5 **WRITING** Choose one of the rules below and use it as a topic for your own 50-word short story.
   - No running in the school corridors.
   - Please pay for your food before you eat it.
   - No swimming in the lake.
   - If you're the last person to leave the room, please turn off the lights.
   - No talking during the examination.
   - Please don't come in unless you are properly dressed.

12 PLAYING BY THE RULES

GRAMMAR
Third conditional

1 Read the example sentences and answer the questions. Then complete the rules.

*If we **had run**, we **wouldn't have missed** the train.*

1 Did they run? Did they miss the train?

*If I **hadn't listened** to my mother, I **wouldn't have got** into trouble.*

2 Did he listen to his mother? Did he get into trouble?

> **RULE:** To talk about unreal situations in the past and their imagined results, we use the third conditional.
> - Condition clause: *If* + ¹_____ .
> - Result clause: *would* (*not*) *have* + ²_____ participle.
>
> The condition clause can come before or after the result clause.

2 Match the parts of the sentences.

1 If I had studied harder, ___
2 If I hadn't studied so much, ___
3 Would she have been late for school ___
4 If she hadn't got up when her alarm rang, ___
5 If we hadn't spent all our money, ___
6 We wouldn't have had enough money to go to the cinema ___

a I wouldn't have passed the test.
b if she had got up when her alarm rang?
c we would have bought him a present.
d the test would have been a lot easier for me.
e if we had spent it all on food.
f she wouldn't have had time for breakfast.

3 Put the verbs into the correct form to make third conditional sentences.

0 If she ___*hadn't been*___ (not be) so rude, I ___*would have helped*___ (help) her.
1 If Paul _____ (not invite) me to his party, I _____ (be) really upset.
2 If she _____ (enter) the competition, I'm sure she _____ (win) it.
3 They _____ (go) in the sea if they _____ (not forget) their swimsuits.
4 We _____ (not win) the game if he _____ (not score) that goal.

4 Read the statement. Imagine a different past and write as many third conditional sentences as you can. Compare your ideas with a partner.

My grandparents met each other. → Workbook page 109

VOCABULARY
Talking about consequences and reasons

1 Match the conversations with the pictures. Write the numbers 1–4.

1 A Why did you stop playing?
  B *Because* it started raining, Mum!
2 A So your parents are angry with you again?
  B Yes. It's *because of* my bad grades at school.
3 A I was really hungry when I got home from school.
  B *That explains why* there aren't any biscuits left in the cupboard.
4 A I forgot to invite Jim to my party.
  B *So that's the reason* he looks so upset.

2 Complete the sentences with your own ideas.

1 A My football team lost again yesterday.
  B That explains why …
2 A I've just come back from a two-week holiday in the US.
  B That's why …
3 A It's my best friend's birthday today.
  B So that's the reason …
4 A Is this your favourite computer game?
  B That's right. It's because of …

→ Workbook page 110

Pronunciation
Silent consonants
Go to page 121.

115

Culture

Strange laws around the world

1 Look at the pictures and answer the questions.

1. Each picture is about a strange law. What do you think the law is for each picture?
2. One person is *not* breaking a strange law. Can you guess which one?

2 Read the blog and do the quiz.

3 Mark the sentences T (true) or F (false).

1. If you steal an alligator, you can go to prison for 12 years. ___
2. The only place that you cannot put a sofa is in the garden. ___
3. A woman who falls asleep under a hair dryer is breaking the law. ___
4. It is a crime to give the king a whale. ___
5. You mustn't start your car if there are children underneath it. ___
6. You can't buy a light bulb yourself. ___

Georgie's blogspot › Weird Laws

The other day someone told me about a very strange law in their country, so I decided to look for more 'weird laws'. When a country brings in a law, it makes sense at the time. Sometimes, however, the law just stays, even when the reason for it has gone.

A lot of different places have laws that we might think are strange. I decided to give you a quiz. Read each law and choose which place (A, B or C) you think the law is from.

Have fun! (The answers are at the bottom, **upside down**.)

1 In _____ , stealing an alligator is against the law. If you steal one, you could **end up** in **prison** for as long as ten years.
   A South Africa   B Louisiana, USA   C Brazil

2 In _____ , if you **own** a sofa, you can put it anywhere you want – **except** in the garden. That's a **crime**!
   A Rio, Brazil   B Colorado, USA
   C Kyoto, Japan

3 In _____ , if the owner of a women's hair salon lets someone fall asleep under a hair dryer, they are **breaking the law**.
   A Britain   B Florida, USA   C France

4 It is **illegal** to chew gum in _____ . If you are caught, you may have to pay a lot of money – and clean the streets!
   A Singapore   B Samoa   C Switzerland

5 In _____ , apparently, you're not allowed to ride a bicycle in a swimming pool.
   A Holland   B Argentina   C California, USA

6 If you're walking on the beach in _____ and find a dead whale, you can't keep it. You have to give it to the queen or king right away.
   A Thailand   B Spain   C Britain

7 In _____ , a law says that before you start your car, you have to check that there are no children asleep underneath it. (What if there are adults?)
   A Denmark   B India   C Australia

8 If you need to change a light bulb in _____ , you have to call an electrician – it's a crime to do it yourself.
   A New York, USA   B Beijing, China
   C Victoria, Australia

12 PLAYING BY THE RULES

4 **SPEAKING** Which of the laws do you think is the funniest? Compare with others in the class.

5 **VOCABULARY** There are eight words and phrases in bold in the texts. Match them with these meanings.

1 doing something that is not allowed _____
2 with the top part at the bottom _____
3 have something that is yours _____
4 something a person does that is not allowed by the government of a country _____
5 arrive (in a place or situation) because of something you did _____
6 a place where criminals are put and they cannot leave _____
7 but not _____
8 against the law _____

WRITING
A set of rules

1 Martha wrote a set of rules for her house and her family for weekends. What does she say about:

1 food?
2 sleep?
3 her room?
4 homework?
5 her sister?
6 school and teachers?
7 TV?
8 herself?

2 Put the words in the correct order to make sentences from Martha's rules. What do the sentences tell you about how she feels about homework, her sister and football?

1 allowed / ask / no one / me / is / homework / about / to
   _____
2 all / isn't / she / at / room / come / allowed / into / to / my
   _____
3 watch / no one / programme / time / at / other / can / any / that
   _____

3 Find the phrases and sentences in Martha's rules that show she isn't 100% serious.

4 Choose one of the sets of rules to write about. Make notes about what you want to include in the rules. (You don't have to be serious, but don't be unkind!)

- A set of rules for your family for the weekend.
- A set of rules for your family for the school holidays.
- A set of rules for you and your family when you go out together (e.g. to the cinema or to a restaurant).
- A set of rules for you and your family when you go somewhere on holiday together.
- A set of rules for … anything you like!

5 Write the set of rules you chose in Exercise 4. Write about 150–180 words. Give them a title. Add some drawings if you want to.

Rules for the weekend at home
1. After school finishes on Friday, Mum and Dad are not allowed to talk to me about school or teachers.
2. Between seven o'clock on Friday evening and nine o'clock on Sunday evening, no one is allowed to ask me about homework. (At other times, they can help me if they want.)
3. No noise before 10 am on Saturday. Saturday is my morning for sleeping.
4. For breakfast on Sunday, I can eat anything I want. Anything at all!!! (And that includes ice-cream!)
5. My sister Juliana is not allowed to use my computer – in fact, she isn't allowed to come into my room at all. (Well, only if she brings chocolate.)
6. My room – I will tidy it late on Sunday, but before then: keep out!
7. If there is a football match on TV with my team, no one can watch any other programme at that time.
8. And lastly – I am not allowed to be boring about rules 1–7!

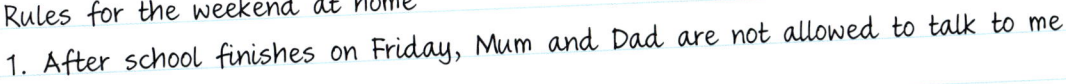

MARTHA (the boss!)

CAMBRIDGE ENGLISH: Preliminary

I THINK EXAMS

READING

Part 1: Three-option multiple choice

Workbook page 71

1 Look at the text in each question. What does it say? Choose the correct letter A, B or C.

1. **Park opening hours 9 am – sunset. Dogs must be on a lead. No ball games**
   - A You can play tennis here.
   - B Dogs are not allowed here.
   - C The park closes before it gets dark.

2. *Hi James, Dave called and asked if you wanted to meet up with him at the weekend. Please call him back when you can. Thanks, Mary*

   Mary tells James
   - A to phone Dave.
   - B to talk to Dave urgently.
   - C to meet Dave at the weekend.

3. **Warning:** This medicine may make you feel sleepy. Do not take before driving a car or using machines.
   - A This medicine is to help you sleep.
   - B It can be dangerous to take this medicine before doing some activities.
   - C Take this medicine if you feel tired at work.

4. *Sorry you weren't there when we called. If you'd been in, we'd have left the parcel. Please collect it from the post office or arrange redelivery on our website.*
   - A You have to go to the post office to get your parcel.
   - B The postman has left your parcel with your neighbour.
   - C You can go online to find a new delivery date.

5. **Free to a good home.** We have six gorgeous Labrador puppies ready for collection in two weeks. Interested in one or two? – Phone Jane on 0203023

   The puppies
   - A can be taken home now.
   - B don't cost anything.
   - C can all go to the same person.

LISTENING

Part 2: Multiple choice

2 🔊 2.36 You will hear a girl called Lucy talking on a TV breakfast show. For each question, choose the correct answer A, B or C.

1. To enter the competition, Lucy had to
   - A make a video of herself and then phone someone.
   - B write a letter and practise reading the weather forecast.
   - C explain why she wanted to win in a letter and send it with a video of herself.

2. What time did Lucy do her weather forecast?
   - A three o'clock
   - B four o'clock
   - C five o'clock

3. How did Lucy feel when she did the forecast?
   - A very excited
   - B excited and a little bit worried
   - C very nervous

4. What was the weather like in the forecast Lucy gave?
   - A There was a variety of types of weather.
   - B It was mainly good for most of the country.
   - C It was cold and snowy.

5. What job does Lucy want to do one day?
   - A She'd like to be on TV.
   - B She'd like to read the weather.
   - C She wants to be a teacher.

TEST YOURSELF   UNITS 11 & 12

VOCABULARY

1 Complete the sentences with the words in the list. There are two extra words.

encouraged | because | because of | explains | fun | told
expected | reason | warned | trouble | funny | behaved

1. I came home late and I got _____ off by my parents.
2. We couldn't go out _____ it was raining.
3. I really didn't like that joke – it just wasn't _____ .
4. I didn't want to do music lessons, but my parents _____ me to give them a try, so I did.
5. Oh, you missed the bus. That _____ why you were late.
6. I'm not surprised you feel ill. I _____ you not to leave the milk out of the fridge!
7. He has lots of problems at school, and he's always getting into _____ .
8. I was surprised when England won. I _____ them to lose.
9. It rained the whole time, so the picnic really wasn't a lot of _____ .
10. I couldn't hear our teacher _____ the noise outside.

/10

GRAMMAR

2 Complete the sentences. Use the correct form of the verbs in the list.

go (x2) | allow | let | not eat (x2)

1. I _____ to the concert if I'd had a ticket.
2. I wanted to go, but my dad didn't _____ me.
3. You would have been OK if you _____ a second hamburger.
4. When I was little, I wasn't _____ to watch TV after eight o'clock.
5. If I'd known it was fish, I _____ it.
6. If everyone _____ to the party, we'd have had a lot more fun.

3 Find and correct the mistake in each sentence.

1. They said me to stay in the house.
2. Why didn't they let me to go home?
3. They wanted me answer some questions.
4. I reminded him to giving me back my book.
5. If I would have known, I wouldn't have told anyone.
6. We hadn't won the game if Graham hadn't played.

/12

FUNCTIONAL LANGUAGE

4 Write the missing words.

1. A I don't understand. Why won't you _____ me read my book?
   B _____ it's nearly midnight, and you have to go to sleep!
2. A It _____ me really angry when people don't tell the truth.
   B I see. So that explains _____ you were cross with Jim.
3. A We aren't _____ to take our mobile phones into class.
   B Oh. So that's the _____ why you didn't phone me.
4. A I _____ it when people shout at me. It's horrible!
   B Well, I wouldn't _____ shouted if you had listened to me the first time!

/8

MY SCORE /30

22 – 30
10 – 21
0 – 9

PRONUNCIATION

UNIT 1
Intonation and sentence stress

1 🔊 1.12 Read and listen to the dialogue.

HENRY   I know … let's learn to **surf**!
LUCY   That's a **great** idea!
HENRY   Do you **think** so?
LUCY   Of course! We'll need **lessons**.
HENRY   I'll phone the **surf shop**!
LUCY   It'll be **fun**… we should **definitely** do it!

2 Which words show that Lucy likes Henry's idea?

3 🔊 1.13 Listen and repeat the dialogue.

UNIT 2
Word stress

1 🔊 1.17 Read and listen to the dialogue.

SARAH   Jack, I can't **believe** it! Do you **recognise** that man over there?
JACK   I **suppose** it could be someone we **know**…
SARAH   How could you **forget**? **Think**, Jack!
JACK   Oh, yeah! Now I **remember**! He's on that TV quiz show.
SARAH   That's right. It's called, '**Concentrate**'. I wonder what he's doing here?

2 How many syllables do the blue / red / green words have? Say these verbs, and stress the correct syllable.

3 🔊 1.18 Listen and repeat the dialogue.

UNIT 3
Words ending in /ə/

1 🔊 1.22 Read and listen to the dialogue.

JOE   Why don't we go to the cinema? We can see The Monst**er** in the Comput**er**. Tammy Bak**er** plays the monst**er**.
TESS Well… there's also Riv**er** Advent**ure**. Tom Webst**er**'s a doct**or** in it.
JOE   I know he's a better act**or** than Tammy Bak**er** but Riv**er** Advent**ure** is a lot long**er**. If we see the short**er** film we can have dinn**er** aft**er**.
TESS Okay; it looks much funni**er**, too. And let's go to the Sup**er** Burg**er** for dinn**er**!

2 Say the words ending in the short /ə/ sound.

3 🔊 1.23 Listen and repeat the dialogue.

UNIT 4
The short /ʌ/ vowel sound

1 🔊 1.31 Read and listen to the poem.

My little c**ou**sin from L**o**ndon's c**o**ming on M**o**nday.
She's y**ou**ng and l**o**vely – and very f**u**nny.
She l**o**ves the s**u**n and r**u**nning and j**u**mping.
She d**oe**sn't like st**u**dying or spending m**o**ney.

2 Say the words with the /ʌ/ vowel sound in blue.

3 🔊 1.32 Listen and repeat the poem.

UNIT 5
been: strong /biːn/ and weak /bɪn/

1 🔊 1.36 Read and listen to the dialogue.

JILL   Where have you **been**? The party's already started.
PETE   Shh! I've **been** hiding in the kitchen.
JILL   We've **been** looking for you everywhere. We want to play a game.
PETE   Well, I've **been** trying to find a bin to put this sandwich in. It's horrible!

2 Say the strong and weak forms of been, /biːn/ and /bɪn/. What other word sounds like /bɪn/?

3 🔊 1.37 Listen and repeat the dialogue.

UNIT 6
/f/, /v/ and /b/ consonant sounds

1 🔊 2.04 Read and listen to the advertisement.

Visit the **b**eautiful **v**illage of **V**ictoria!
The **v**illage is surrounded **b**y **f**orests and **f**arms.
There's a **f**antastic ri**v**er for **f**ishing.
You can **b**uy sou**v**enirs and see **v**ery old **b**uildings.
There are **b**uses to the **b**each **f**rom Monday to **F**riday.
You'll ne**v**er **f**orget your **v**isit to **V**ictoria!

2 Say the words with the /f/, /v/ and /b/ sounds.

3 🔊 2.05 Listen and repeat the sentences.

PRONUNCIATION

UNIT 7
Intonation of question tags

1 🔊 **2.08** Read and listen to the dialogue.

SAM You do want to come, *don't you?*
MAX I'm not sure. Jane's got those big dogs, *hasn't she?*
SAM Yes, they're enormous! But they're very friendly.
MAX Well I don't like dogs, *do I?*
SAM You're not afraid, *are you?*
MAX Of course not!

2 Look at the blue question tags. Circle the correct words in each sentence.

Sam *knows / doesn't know* the answer to his questions. His voice goes *up / down*.

Now look at the red question tags. Circle the correct words in each sentence.

Max *knows / doesn't know* the answer to his questions. His voice goes *up / down*.

3 🔊 **2.09** Listen and repeat the dialogue.

UNIT 8
The /juː/ sound

1 🔊 **2.13** Read and listen to the dialogue.

TEACHER Hello St**ew**art! How are **you**? **You u**sed to be one of my best st**u**dents!
STEWART Hello, Mrs Jones. I'm studying m**u**sic and comp**u**ting at **u**niversity now.
TEACHER M**u**sic and comp**u**ting! Isn't that an un**u**sual combination?
STEWART Not really. In the f**u**ture I'd like to write m**u**sic programs for comp**u**ters. It's really n**ew** technology and very exciting.

2 Say the words with the /juː/ sound.

3 🔊 **2.14** Listen and repeat the dialogue.

UNIT 9
/tʃ/ and /dʒ/ consonant sounds

1 🔊 **2.17** Read and listen to the dialogue.

CHARLIE If I could be anything, I'd **ch**oose to be a **j**ournalist. What about you, **J**ane?
JANE **J**ournalism's a very dan**g**erous **j**ob, **Ch**arlie. I'm going to be a **ch**ess player.
CHARLIE You've **ch**anged your mind! You wanted to be a **G**eography tea**ch**er.
JANE Yes. I've just **j**oined a **ch**ess club. My coa**ch** thinks I've got a good **ch**ance of becoming a **ch**ampion.

2 Say the words with the /tʃ/ and /dʒ/ sounds.

3 🔊 **2.18** Listen and repeat the dialogue.

UNIT 10
/tʃ/ and /ʃ/ consonant sounds

1 🔊 **2.23** Read and listen to the dialogue.

PAT Welcome to the **sh**ow. We're in the ki**tch**en today with our **ch**ef, Mi**tch**ell.
MITCH Hello. In this demonstra**t**ion I'm making a spe**c**ial Ru**ss**ian di**sh**.
PAT Wa**tch** carefully as our **Ch**ef Mi**tch**ell makes the di**sh** you see in this pic**t**ure.
MITCH Patri**c**ia, please put the oven at the right tempera**t**ure while I **ch**op the **ch**erries… now we add the **s**ugar – but you **sh**ouldn't use too mu**ch**! And now it's ready to bake.
PAT And here's a fini**sh**ed one! It tastes deli**c**ious!

2 Say the words with the /ʃ/ and /tʃ/ sounds.

3 🔊 **2.24** Listen and repeat the dialogue.

UNIT 11
Intonation: rude or polite?

1 🔊 **2.29** Read and listen to the dialogue.

CLERK Could you put that bag down over there, please.
MR YOUNG Excuse me. Could you repeat that?
CLERK Yes, could you put that bag down over there!
MR YOUNG I mean, could you repeat that *politely*?
CLERK I'm *terribly* sorry. Could you put that bag down over there, please.

2 Which sentences sound rude? Which polite?

3 🔊 **2.30** Listen and repeat the dialogue.

UNIT 12
Silent consonants

1 🔊 **2.34** Read and listen to the dialogue.

GUARD 1 Shh! Lis**t**en! Someone's ta**l**king in the next room.
GUARD 2 Yes, and at this **h**our the cas**t**le shou**l**d be emp**t**y.
GUARD 1 We shou**l**d investigate. Or, erm, shou**l**d we **w**rite a report?
GUARD 2 I can't answer that. All I **k**now is that we mus**t**n't stay here another minute!

2 Say the words with the silent consonants in blue.

3 🔊 **2.35** Listen and repeat the dialogue.

GET IT RIGHT!

UNIT 1
Present perfect vs. past simple

> Learners often use the present perfect when the past simple is required.
>
> We use the past simple to talk about events which have taken place at a specific time. We use the present perfect to talk about events where the time is not specified.
>
> ✓ I **went** on holiday with my family last year.
> ✗ I ~~have been~~ on holiday with my family last year.

Write positive answers to the following questions using the words given in the correct tense.

0   Have you started your new job? (last weekend)
    Yes, I have. I started my new job last weekend.

1   Have you seen the latest episode? (yesterday)

2   Have you been to France before? (two times)

3   Have you visited your grandparents recently? (a few days ago)

4   Have you seen John? (five minutes ago)

5   Have you changed your phone? (for a better one)

6   Have you earned any money recently? (over £100 last week)

UNIT 2
Present perfect with *for* or *since*

> Learners often use the present simple with *for* or *since* when the present perfect is required.
>
> We use the present perfect tense with both *for* and *since* referring to an earlier time which is still relevant now.
>
> ✓ I **have known** him for three months.
> ✗ I ~~know~~ him for three months.

Make new sentences in the perfect tense using the information given.

0   I started playing the guitar when I was six years old. I still play the guitar now.
    I've played the guitar since I was six years old.

1   We were friends when we were ten. We are still friends now.

2   I saw her when I was five. I did not see her after that.

3   I started working in the newsagent's two years ago. I work there now.

4   You moved to Madrid six months ago.

5   My family travelled abroad in 2010. They did not travel abroad after that.

6   Have you earned any money recently? (over £100 last week)

UNIT 3
Comparatives and *than*

> Learners often use the wrong forms of adjectives, trying to use *more* where it is not possible, especially with *bigger* and *cheaper*.
>
> For adjectives with one syllable, we add *-er* for the comparative.
>
> ✓ In ten years' time my town will be **bigger** than now.
> ✗ In ten years' time my town will be ~~more big~~ than now.
>
> For adjectives with two syllables ending in *-y*, we make the comparative by adding *-ier*.
>
> ✓ I find English **easier** than French.
> ✗ I find English ~~more easy~~ than French.
>
> Learners sometimes use *that* instead of *than*.
>
> ✓ Sports clubs are much better **than** the gym.
> ✗ Sports clubs are much better ~~that~~ the gym.

GET IT RIGHT!

Correct the following sentences.

1 I am much more happy than before.

2 If you go to Europe, the weather will be better in July that in February.

3 Which is more old, soccer or rugby?

4 The beaches are cleaner in the countryside that in the city.

5 It will make you fitter and more healthy.

UNIT 4
Any vs. – (no article)

> Learners often miss out *any* where it is needed in questions and negative statements.
> ✓ Do you have **any** questions? If so, please visit me in my office.
> ✗ Do you have ___ questions? If so, please visit me in my office.

Circle the correct answer, *any* or – (no article).

1 In the countryside there aren't *any* / – discos.
2 I didn't take *any* / – notice of it and deleted it again.
3 I have been doing *any* / – homework.
4 We need *any* / – time to work on this.
5 I have been here for four months and I can't live here *any* / – longer.
6 Do you have *any* / – money I can borrow?

will vs. *should*

> Learners sometimes use *will* instead of *should*.
>
> We use *should* to give advice to someone, or to mean that something is supposed to happen.
> ✓ In my opinion, the subject you **should** talk about is the environment.
> ✗ In my opinion, the subject you ~~will~~ talk about is the environment.

Circle the correct answer.

1 In my opinion, you *will* / *should* not move schools.
2 If you like the seaside, you *will* / *should* go to the south coast.
3 If we do it that way, it *will* / *should* be a disaster.
4 On this diet, you must eat healthy food, and you *won't* / *shouldn't* drink fizzy drinks.
5 *I'll* / *I should* meet you there if you like.
6 *Will* / *Should* we study everything for the test or just this unit?

UNIT 5
Present simple or present continuous vs. present perfect continuous

> Learners sometimes use the present simple or the present continuous when the present perfect continuous is required.
>
> We use the present perfect continuous to talk about how long we have been doing something. We often use it with *for* and *since* and a time period.
> ✓ I **have been living** in this house for three years.
> ✗ I ~~live~~ in this house for three years.
> ✓ I ~~am living~~ in this house for three years.

Correct the following sentences.

1 I try to do that for ages, but I can't manage it.

2 How long is Michael learning English?

3 I have always been going to work by train, because I live far away.

4 His friends laugh every time he is telling that joke – I don't know why.

5 I need to fill in your address – where have you been living?

6 Since last Wednesday I go to karate lessons.

123

UNIT 6
Future with *will*

> **Learners sometimes use the present simple tense when the future tense is required.**
> ✓ We **will meet** at 9 p.m. tomorrow.
> ✗ We ~~meet~~ at 9 p.m. tomorrow.

Correct the following sentences.

1 We normally will go there every Wednesday.
   _____

2 I think I will know what you mean.
   _____

3 So I see you on the 15th.
   _____

4 I'm sure you want to go there when you see these pictures.
   _____

5 When I will get home, I'll send you a text.
   _____

6 Who wins the next football match?
   _____

UNIT 7
Future forms and time phrases

> **Learners sometimes use the wrong word order with time phrases.**
>
> **We put the time phrase after the verbs and object phrases.**
> ✓ I hope you will come **with me next year**.
> ✗ I hope you will come ~~next year with me~~.

Correct the following sentences.

1 He will look this week at my project.
   _____

2 I can't straight away help you, but I will as soon as I can.
   _____

3 I'll do immediately what you've suggested.
   _____

4 Will you by Friday have it finished?
   _____

5 I will talk now to him.
   _____

6 I bet he won't next time do it like that.
   _____

Question tags

> **Learners sometimes use the wrong verb in the tag question.**
>
> **We form question tags by using the same verb if the verb is an auxiliary (*be*, *have*) or modal verb (*can*, *will*, *would*, etc.), but we use *do* with all other verbs.**
>
> **We use a pronoun which agrees with the subject of the verb, and we keep the tense the same.**
> ✓ He played the whole game, **didn't he**?
> ✗ He played the whole game, ~~isn't it~~?

Correct the following question tags.

0 This is a good idea, doesn't it?
   This is a good idea, isn't it?

1 He is working on his project, doesn't he?
   _____

2 We have always wanted to travel, don't we?
   _____

3 That doesn't sound very interesting, is it?
   _____

4 You don't finish work at 6 p.m., are you?
   _____

5 It would probably be too far to walk there, isn't it?
   _____

6 He's driving much too fast on these wet roads, doesn't he?
   _____

UNIT 8
used to vs. *usually*

> **Learners sometimes confuse *used to* with *usually*.**
>
> **We use *used to* to indicate an action that was happening regularly in the past but not now, while *usually* means any action that has happened or is happening regularly.**
> ✓ When I have some spare time, I **usually** go running in the park.
> ✗ When I have some spare time, I ~~used to~~ go running in the park.

GET IT RIGHT!

Complete the sentences with *used to* or *usually*.

0 When I was younger, I _used to_ go skiing with my family.
1 If I have time, I _____ play computer games in the evening.
2 When I was younger I _____ listen to pop music all the time.
3 They _____ hang out every Saturday night so that's when I see them.
4 We _____ buy clothes twice a year, but now that we have extra money we go shopping more often.
5 Now that I go to the tennis club, I _____ get home late.
6 I _____ go on camping holidays, but that was a long time ago.

Second conditional tenses

> Learners sometimes use the wrong tenses in the clauses of the second conditional.
>
> We form the second conditional by using the past simple tense in the *if* clause, and the *would* form in the main clause.
> ✓ If I **knew** what to do, I would do it.
> ✗ If I ~~would know~~ what to do, I would do it.

Correct the following sentences.

1 If you answered my email I will be very pleased.

2 It would be fantastic if you would come to visit me.

3 If I find your mobile, I would bring it on Monday

4 I am very grateful if you could meet me at 11 on Sunday.

5 If I broke this vase, my parents will be angry.

6 I will love it if you could visit me in the holidays.

UNIT 9
Present simple passive vs. past simple passive

> Learners sometimes confuse the present simple passive with the past simple passive.
>
> We use the past simple passive to refer to events which took place in the past.
> ✓ I **was** really surprised when I first read the email.
> ✗ I ~~am~~ really surprised when I first read the email.
>
> We use the present simple passive for events which have started and are still going on now.
> ✓ We'll go to Paris in two weeks – the tickets **are** booked.
> ✗ We'll go to Paris in two weeks – the tickets ~~were~~ booked.

Correct the following sentences.

1 I always keep shopping until the mall was closed.

2 I am born in Britain and have lived here since then.

3 I'm proud that my town is chosen as City of Culture.

4 The hotel was located in front of the beach, so that will be very convenient.

5 Ten minutes later my tent is flooded and I had to leave it because everything was wet.

6 I am given a puppy for my last birthday.

UNIT 10
Past perfect vs. past simple

> Learners often confuse the past perfect with the past simple.
>
> We use the past perfect tense to refer to events which happened at an earlier point in the past, compared with another past event. We use the past simple for an event which occurred generally in the past.
> ✓ By the time I got there, he **had left**.
> ✗ By the time I got there, he ~~left~~.

Rewrite the sentences using the correct form of the verb in brackets.

0 The trip was awesome because I (dream) about it all my life.
   The trip was awesome because I had dreamed about it all my life.

1 Our PE teacher taught us the rules of tennis and we (start) to play.

2 I (come) home from school when it happened.

3 I didn't give the teacher my homework yesterday because I (leave) my bag at home.

4 When we had finished eating and drinking we (go) for a walk in the town centre.

5 Do you like these jeans? I (buy) them yesterday.

6 The letter was from Brown University – they (accept) me!

UNIT 11
say vs. tell

> **Learners often confuse *say* and *tell* when reporting speech.**
>
> **We tell someone (something).**
> ✓ I **told** her I was coming to Italy.
> ✗ I ~~said~~ her I was coming to Italy.
>
> **We say something (to someone).**
> ✓ I **said** I would go this Summer.
> ✗ I ~~told~~ I would go this Summer.

Write a cross (✗) next to the incorrect sentences. Then write the correct sentences.

0 He said me to wait, so I did. ✗
   He told me to wait, so I did.

1 My parents told that you can come along.

2 She told me to order her a pepperoni pizza.

3 As they told, it is a very big sports centre with a lot of facilities.

4 I want to say you about this great new computer game.

5 I don't know who I can say about this problem.

6 She asked me to talk about me and my life.

7 Did you say her on what day and at what time she has to be here?

8 The customer has made a complaint – he tells that his order hasn't arrived yet.

UNIT 12
let vs. make

> **Learners often confuse when to use *let* and when to use *make*.**
>
> **We use *let* to indicate that someone is allowed to do something.**
> ✓ She **let** them have as much ice cream as they wanted.
> ✗ She ~~made~~ them have as much ice cream as they wanted.
>
> **We use *make* to indicate that something or someone is the cause of something.**
> ✓ The sweet song **made** us all cry.
> ✗ The sweet song ~~let~~ us all cry.

Circle the correct answer.

1 You can go ahead – I won't *let / make* you wait for me.
2 *Let / Make* me ask you something – do you have any plans for Saturday?
3 Could you *let / make* her know I'll be late?
4 That document really *lets / makes* you think about the problems caused by pollution.
5 They can't *let / make* us stay late if we don't want to.
6 If you help me tidy the house and prepare the food, I'll *let / make* you invite your friends to the party, too.

STUDENT A

UNIT 1, PAGE 19

Student A

1. You've got an idea of how to raise money for a charity in India: Students can pay £1 and not wear their school uniform one day next week. But is it really a good idea? You're not too sure. Tell Student B your idea and see what they think.
2. Student B wants to tell you about an idea for a new school club. Listen to the idea and encourage them to do it. Offer help and maybe some ideas of your own.

UNIT 5, PAGE 55

Student A

1. You're a bit upset. There's a party at the weekend, but your mum says you can't go. Talk to your friend about the problem.
2. Your friend looks a bit upset. Find out what the problem is and see if you can help.
   Why don't you …
   You could …
   Can't you … ?

UNIT 9, PAGE 91

Student A

1. You and some friends are going to the cinema. See if Student B wants to come.
2. Student B invites you to do something with a group of friends. You want to do it.

STUDENT B

UNIT 1, PAGE 19

Student B

1. Student A wants to tell you about an idea to raise money for a charity in India. Listen to the idea and encourage them to do it. Offer help and maybe some ideas of your own.
2. You've got an idea for a new school club: a cooking club that helps students learn how to cook healthy food. But is it really a good idea? You're not too sure. Tell Student B your idea and see what they think.

UNIT 5, PAGE 55

Student B

1. Your friend looks a bit upset. Find out what the problem is and see if you can help.

   Why don't you …
   You could …
   Can't you … ?

2. You're a bit upset. It's your mum's birthday tomorrow and you haven't got any money to buy her a present. Talk to your friend about the problem.

UNIT 9, PAGE 91

Student B

1. Student A invites you to do something with a group of friends. You can't do it. Say why you can't.
2. You and some friends are going for a long walk. See if Student A wants to come.